WOMAN:

HER DIGNITY AND SPHERE.

BY A LADY.

PUBLISHED BY THE
AMERICAN TRACT SOCIETY,
150 NASSAU-STREET, NEW YORK.

Contents

WOMAN:

HER DIGNITY AND SPHERE.

LIVING in an age of unparalleled activity, the capabilities and resources of man seemingly unlimited—an age of revolution, crowned heads swept into obscurity, and Liberty sitting at ease in the halls of despotism; old theories, as old dynasties, passing into oblivion; new forms, new views, new ideas, new systems, new combinations coming and going, meeting and mingling—an age when the public mind is agitated with strange and intricate questions; the vital forces of good and evil waging a mighty warfare; speculation making bold advances, imagination running riot with reason—an age when the legitimate rights and equality of the sexes are made the topic of the hour; when the dignity of woman is assailed, her sphere of action discussed, her motives suspected, her capabilities analyzed, one crying out that she has too little to do, and another asking, what more can she do?—it becomes us to pause and ask ourselves, not for the purpose of discussion, but as the most simple and direct way of arriving at the truth, what part or lot have we in this advance movement? Are we standing at our posts, faithful in the service given us to do, valiant to do battle against wrong, or are we stragglers loitering behind, a prey to the enemy, a reproach to our Leader?

Examples are not wanting to show that a question simply put, has a tendency to rouse into activity the faculties and affections of the mind, and not unfrequently, to change the purpose and the character. If the simple questions we incline to ask should lead a minority of our sisters to pause and reflect before they answer, the purpose that we have in view will be accomplished—the object of this little work fully met.

But lest some one about to cross on the plank of expediency becomes confused and dizzy as she questions her own individual aim and purpose, asking with all humility, What can I do? we would whisper, Nothing but what God has given you the ability to perform; or in other words, Any thing that you can do, and do well.

"God said, Let us make man in our image, after our likeness; and let them have dominion—so God created man in his own image, in the image of God created he him: male and female created he them." The singular and the plural here used, and likewise male and female, show equality, with essential differences of temperament and constitution, out of which must of necessity arise distinct characteristics and individual duties.

It is with reference to these distinctive duties that speculations have arisen, and theories have been shaped, to puzzle heads wise and unwise. We do not propose to map out for woman a new path, neither to combat nor annul popular error. We would simply and unostentatiously hold up the pattern given of God, and we would in all humility ask, Is this the standard to which womanly perfection is now verging, and by what means can the channel of her usefulness be deepened, her influence extended?

But I hear it whispered, "Woman's duties have changed materially; they are ten to one to what they were fifty years ago." Yet if her duties have increased, it does not change her nature, nor dim the lustre of her individuality; she must act, necessity is laid upon her. And if woman is necessitated to exert herself, this necessity is known and permitted of God, and always for a wise purpose. Our heavenly Father does not require of his creatures what he has not given them the ability to perform.

It is said with truth, that woman owes every thing to Christianity. In former times, among the lower classes, woman was little more than a beast of burden; in the upper circles she was carefully guarded and tenderly treated, her beauty increased by the costliest robes and most brilliant jewels; for her sake knights fought and champions died; set up for a prize she was won by the bravest: not as a companion, but as a choice possession, to be petted for a season and then laid aside. Where gospel privileges are not known, her position now is much the same, but where Christian influence is felt, she has ever been the first to acknowledge it; and while it has moulded and developed her to an equality with man, to be his adviser, his co-worker, his loved and loving companion, it has deprived her of none of her charms, but has, on the other hand, greatly increased them. Like all radical changes, this has been the work of time—a gradual elevation of character and position; and it is not yet perfected, neither will it be until the majority of thinking women realize that they are created for something more than enjoyment, understand something of their own powers, and honestly strive to exert those powers to the full extent, in the furtherance of truth and goodness in the world.

It is a serious question, as the mother looks upon the little nestlings gathered at her knee, and asks, "What is the great object of a girl's education? What is the end and aim of her life?" Looking upon our little ones, our thoughts running out into the unknown future, the question comes to us as mothers, Cannot we teach them that work is noble, that a true development of body and mind is the result of effort; that enjoyment is never so satisfying as when it follows in the wake of duty? Can we not teach them to be frank without being immodest; to be free without being extravagant; to be helpful without being patronizing; to be economical without stinginess? Can we not teach them the higher law, without losing sight of the little amenities of social life—the charms and graces, the little pleasant ways that render girlhood so lovely?

The sculptor, in his studio, chips and chisels and moulds according to the ideal before him. The block of marble is to him something more than a block of marble; he looks and studies, he thinks and feels, and realizes the presence of the angel there. He sees it, and he works incessantly, that he may reveal it to the gaze of others. Is it not thus as we look upon the lovely child committed to our care, an inhabitant of our workshop, to be moulded, shaped, polished? Every blow of the sculptor has a direct bearing upon the future, he does not think to perfect his work in a day; he chips and chisels, and studies his model—it is his life work; his energies are taxed, his judgment brought into requisition, his entire being absorbed in bringing out and developing a form of loveliness fitted to awake and foster sentiments of pity, love, compassion, or high and lofty purpose in the heart of the beholder. A faint portraiture this of the mother's work, "line upon line, precept upon precept, here a little and there a little," moulding and shaping—while each word and look and act has a direct bearing upon the future—not a block of senseless marble, but a human soul, the beauty or the deformity of which is to be developed through her instrumentality.

The sculptor does not fashion his block having a preconceived idea in his mind of the exact place and position whence it will be viewed: he aims to make it perfect, and this achieved, he knows that it will be fitted to inspire the beholder with the same sentiments; that it will prove to be of value in any place or locality where it may be set up.

In the education of our daughters are

we not to follow the same plan? We have no inherited rights and inalienable possessions: fortunes are unstable; farmers become merchants; artisans become lawyers; laborers become judges and divines; rich men's daughters become the wives of poor men, and the reverse. Let education, therefore, be as broad and general as possible. Discipline, strength, knowledge, are useful in every position; for herself should a girl be educated, not to make her a skilful musician, an amateur artist, a passable linguist; but to render her a strong, wise, sensible woman, with a firm, pure principle of right in her heart. Secure this, and she will grace any position, and be ready for every duty.

But the objection has been made, and may be made again, that much study is not required of a woman. If it is needful for a boy to study, delving at Greek and Latin roots; searching through the labyrinths of metaphysics, tangling his brains with mathematics; dissecting, analyzing, and discussing, for the sole purpose of training and strengthening his intellect, laying the foundation for a noble manhood, is it less necessary that his sister should have the benefit of study and discipline, to fit her for a noble womanhood? Ought a sister, wife, mother, to have less discipline for the battle of life, than a brother, son, husband? Does any one fear that the woman, eating of the tree of knowledge, will become too wise, discerning good and evil? Knowledge with love, puffeth not up, neither is it unseemly: rightly educate a woman, and there is little danger of her falling into forbidden paths. It is the smatterer that becomes giddy and falls. Compact knowledge, like the ballast in a ship, leads to security.

Neither will the like amount of study render the girl masculine, any more than it will render the boy effeminate. Let the sister and the brother take the same college course, and through the length and breadth of daily study and research, the characteristics of each will be manifest. Mental development will not be the same, any more than physical habit and formation; the one still a girl, light, graceful, loved, the other shy, backward, and ill at ease, his boyishness a more ungrateful garment than his sister's girlhood.

The word education covers more than a college course, however. In the years usually given to study, lessons are learned from the surroundings and circumstances of life, as well as from books. The sculptor, in the beginning, makes broad lines and chips freely, but as he advances he is more cautious; a deep cut will mar his work; he looks closely; the glancing of his chisel a hair's breadth will change the expression, the slightest deviation will affect the success of all his toil. Thus, while books and the discipline of study are needful, answering to broad lines and free chippings, moulding and giving shape, the expression is the effect of right principle continually exerted and never lost sight of; the outgrowth of home influence, without which mere books will not suffice to educate.

Another object in study is thoroughness; an aim and a purpose, practical and available if need be. Life is uncertain; the brightest hopes may fail; the most flattering prospects elude our grasp. A thorough understanding of branches pursued will be so much capital, profitable under any circumstances, and sure to be a source of satisfaction if the skies are dark and lowering.

It is not unusual to hear it said of woman, that she lacks aim, going with the tide, drifting, swayed, beaten, without well-directed purpose. If this is so, is it not the effect of education? Can we not, as mothers, correct this tendency in our own daughters? Cannot we teach them that it is as disreputable for a woman to be listless, idle, aimless, as it is for a young man to have no regular business.

If this reproach is and has been true in the main, there are and have been manifold wives and mothers that have nobly stood at the helm, braving the storms of life, and eventually landing their precious cargo in a safe harbor. All honor to such women, the meed of a higher praise awaits them than we can give. Our aim is to swell the number of those who find it their highest delight to mould and polish the jewels committed to their trust, working and waiting for results sure to come in the higher life attained, the noble manhood and womanhood of their children. Could an angel ask higher service than God himself has given woman, permitting her to be the sharer and co-worker with man, hastening the end for which he toils, sustaining him by her counsel, strengthening him by her love, making his home a resting-place, whence he is to emerge with armor bright and glistening.

Many a young man has been saved to himself and to the world by the gentle ministrations of a loving sister. Many a father saved from despair by the timely aid of a daughter on whom he had bestowed a careful culture, one who had so improved her privileges, that when the dark hour came she was able and willing to aid him in his business, and by this means secure to him a home in his age and helplessness. There are others who cheerfully stifle every thought of self, giving themselves to incessant toil in order to educate and bring up a family of orphan brothers and sisters. The records of such lives may not be made manifest here, but they are bright in heaven.

It is no doubt to teach us what woman is capable of doing, that so many shrinking, sensitive ones are left to do for themselves and for others. We should never know the beauty of the stars but for night and darkness; and woman's nature cannot be seen in all its beauty, until the winds of adversity have blown away the tinsel and glare by which she was surrounded. Diamonds are found in solitude, and the jewels of the mind only become more precious when viewed by themselves, independent of their setting.

Should it not be the aim of woman to

use her abilities to the best purpose in whatever position God has placed her, using her privileges as stepping-stones; lifting up her own life and generously aiding others, who, perchance have not received as bountifully? In view of her individual accountability, ought not every woman to let her influence reflect only the true, the beautiful, and the good, doing whatsoever her hands find to do; thinking it the highest honor to be a woman, a mother, to fashion, to mould, and to polish jewels for the kingdom of her God? And still, as mothers, is it not necessary that our minds be stirred in reference to the homely lessons needful every day, simple and unpretending, but all-important, the groundwork of all that is noble and good here, of all that is bright and glorious hereafter?

I.

Truthfulness.

IT is said of one of the ancient kings, that he had a mirror into which he was accustomed to look, when called to decide upon important matters connected with his government and the well being of his people. It was well for this ancient king, and well for his people, that he was blessed with a mirror, the simple looking into which enabled him to dispense justice, to decide with wisdom, and to dictate such laws as should be for the furtherance of the public good. We are not told that any one but the king was in possession of such a treasure. Unlike the people under this ancient king, such a mirror has been given to each one of us—a mirror of truth that reflects the way and the manner so perfectly, that by looking into it in all cases in which a decision is to be made touching ourselves, or in reference to others, we are enabled to know our duty.

Such a treasure is given to us mothers; and if the possession caused the heart of the old king to rejoice, how much more do our hearts overflow with gratitude—as we look into the sweet child faces committed to our keeping, and think of our responsibility with regard to them—to be able to inquire of it continually, "How shall we order the child? How shall we do unto him?"

Looking into the mirror of God's word, we find that first impressions are lasting. With our little ones clinging to our knees, we look into this mirror and find that children were brought to Christ by their mothers, that He blessed them, and said, "Suffer little children to come," meaning that they were to come through all time. We see the mothers leading up their little ones to be blessed of God, and thus we are taught to lead up our children for his blessing, even when they are babes in our arms drawing nourishment from our bosoms. Neither is it sufficient to lead them to Christ; they must be taught, trained for him, "that our sons may be as plants grown up in their youth; that our daughters may be as cornerstones, polished after the similitude of a palace." This process of polishing is essentially the mother's. The character of the child is yet unformed, the smooth tablet of the heart is free of outward impression. What characters are to be written there? What impressions made? What influences brought to bear upon them?

Holding up the mirror, we are enabled to see that TRUTHFULNESS is the first lesson to be written there. By this we do not mean the merely opposite of what is false, but the truth in all things, according to their capacity to receive it. Let them see from the outset, that "life is real, life is earnest," and that "death is not the goal." "Even a child is known by his doings, whether his work be pure, and whether it be right." How sweet to feel the little clinging fingers, the serious look that creeps over their rosy dimpled faces, as they make an attempt to look for themselves into this wonderful mirror. Children are strangely imitative; what they see others do, that they are inclined to attempt. The little girl just beginning to totter over the floor, presses her doll to her bosom, hushes and rocks it precisely as she has seen her mother or her nurse hush the baby sister. To play with dolls is innate and perfectly natural; some one says she cannot help it. True, it is in keeping with her nature; but a phase of her nature that would not have developed itself. Had she not seen it done, she would not have originated it.

Not alone nursing dolls, but in "making believe to keep house," the little girl uses the look, walk, and manner, using the very words: small things, it may be said, but the very things that go to prove the necessity, as mothers, of being true to ourselves, true to our principles, our love of the good and the beautiful reflected in the lives of our little ones. An eminent divine was once asked how old a child must be before there was reasonable hope of its being a Christian. "Age has nothing to do with it," was the answer; "love to Jesus, trust, repose, confidence, are all qualities that agree with the child's nature. As soon as the child can understand to love and trust his mother, then can he love and trust Jesus. As the Friend of his mother, Jesus will be his friend, loved and honored."

Is not this true? And if true, can we be too careful? These little imitators looking to us morning, noon, and night, bowing with us in supplication, we need God's blessing on each act, as well as on the food we eat—making our religion practical in our homes, with nothing dark, cold, and stern, but warm, loving, genial; looking to Jesus as a personal friend, leaning upon him, talking with him and of him just as we talk with and of a beloved earthly friend, going to him in times of trouble, in sorrow, and distress; making him the sharer of our joy, the one in whom we think, and move, and feel, the Beloved whose presence is the joy of our souls.

We all know how easy it is for our children to love their relatives, grandparents, uncles, aunts, cousins; the little reverential air on their laughing faces, as they take the letters in their chubby fingers, kissing the pictured semblance of the distant loved one; sending messages as we write, asking questions, and interested to the forgetfulness of play. Would this be so if they were less imitative, less inclined to do as we do, to trust as we trust, to love as we love? And if this is so, cannot we incline them to love with an abiding love things lovely and of good report?

Is it not a mistake to think a child, because he is a child, must be petted, fondled, and put aside as a toy; or eluded as a hinderance, an obstacle in the way of enjoyment? All the while the little active brain is drinking in knowledge; and the heart is like a roll of spotless canvas on which pictures are to be painted, if not by the mother, then by the hand of another, for pictures will be there.

A mother, whose daughters were the pride and the ornament of her house, being asked what was the secret of her success in the education of her children, replied: "From the first time I held them in my arms, I endeavored to make them my friends, my companions as well as my children. I let them see my love for them, my interest in them; I studied their habits, character, temperament; how to benefit them was the one aim of my life. Loving Jesus, I taught them to love him, and in all our daily intercourse I was careful to be true to myself, true to my Christian profession, faithfully striving in my own life and walk to set them an example that they could safely follow."

The Bible says: "Train up a child in the way he should go, and when he is old he will not depart from it." Childhood is the time to lay foundations. Principles of truth implanted in the heart of a child must have an effect upon his future. Samuel was given to God in his infancy; Timothy was taught from a child to fear the Lord; "the unfeigned faith which dwelt first in thy grandmother Lois, and thy mother Eunice; and I am persuaded that in thee also."

In this Paul gives us to understand the teaching given to Timothy, and the fruits of it as seen in his life—"the unfeigned faith." If truthfulness is inculcated, there must be nothing feigned, no deception, however harmless it may be at the time considered. An English divine being at the house of a lady who was desirous of spending the evening with a friend, overheard her planning how to deceive her little daughter, so as to have the satisfaction of knowing that the child was asleep before she left the house. "I will just put on my cap and lie down beside her, and she will think that I am going to sleep."

"Madam," said the clergyman, as the lady appeared before him, "would you like your little daughter to grow up a liar?"

The abruptness of the question, as well as the horror connected with the thought, caused the lady to burst into tears.

"Oh, no, sir; it would kill me to have my child become such a character."

"Then do not set her the example. If you deceive her now, what security have you that she will not deceive you when she comes to act for herself?"

"I had not thought any thing of this kind; my child is so young," stammered the lady.

"Young as your child is, she is old enough to know the difference between reality and pretence. Do not permit your child to learn deception from her mother."

The expression of the face not unfrequently gives the idea of deception as readily as words, saying one thing and looking another. If we would bring up our daughters to be as "cornerstones, polished after the similitude of a palace," we must not weaken their faith, and dim the lustre of their confidence in us, by the use of deception in word or deed.

Looking into this mirror continually, keeps bright the links of parental relationship; each child a special gift, a trust from God, an immortal mind to be developed, a heart to be cultured, a soul to be fitted for the service of God here, an inhabitant of heaven hereafter. Prying little eyes looking into out-of-the-way corners, now is the time to set before them all lovely pictures. How sweet it is to see the light of an awakened understanding breaking over their gleeful faces, the curious gaze deepening into absolute wonder. Now is the time to make the impression, stamping in truthfulness what the favor and glitter of life can never destroy. No after power is superior to the influence of a mother in infancy. It is from us that the child receives the most abiding and far-reaching impressions.

In view of this, can we look into the mirror too frequently? Can we consult it too carefully, studying the requirements laid down in His word, suiting them in measure to the infant capacity, line upon line, precept upon precept? "Thou shalt teach them diligently unto thy children, and shalt talk of them when thou sittest in thy house, and when thou walkest by the way, and when thou liest down, and when thou risest up." Again, "Bring them up in the nurture and admonition of the Lord." Plainly then, this is a personal duty, a duty that it is the privilege of the mother to take to herself. Blessed privilege! to sit with our children on our knees, stringing pearls and weaving cloth of gold, to be fashioned and worn after we have passed away. Starry eyes, dimpled mouths and chubby clinging fingers, jewels given for our adorning, will ye ever be more beautiful, more dearly prized? Which of us can forget the thrill of happiness when invested for the first time with the sacred name of mother! Is there a joy on earth to equal it? Is there a glory to be compared to it? Is there place or position for which she would exchange it?

This joy, that floods our souls as the great sea fills the laughing pools that dimple the rocky shore, is to be reflected in the bright, genial home: making it a paradise for our children, its daily beauty to outshine what may be found outside. To realize this, great expenditure is unnecessary. Magnificent dwellings, large rooms and costly furniture, do not of necessity make a happy home. My neighbor over the way has all these, but there are no little pattering footsteps in her hall, no silvery voices to waken her in the morning, no ringing laughter to echo through the stately rooms, no gleeful little faces, no loving hand-clasp, no white, dimpled arms to cling around her neck. My neighbor keeps her carriage, and down the marble steps she floats in silks and laces; the prancing bays and glittering carriage make a pretty show; and holding my baby up to look, she laughs and crows, patting my face, and murmuring, "Mamma." My neighbor looks and sighs. I know she 'd give it all to feel the little clinging arms about her neck, the tiny rosebud mouth pressed to her own. What care I for silks and laces! my gown is neat and trim, my collar white and smooth—and my baby, my crown, my pearl, my jewel, outshines my neighbor's wealth.

Two gardeners my neighbor keeps, with ample grounds full of rare plants and sweetly perfumed flowers. Statues gleam through the rift of leaves, and fountains flash, with marble basins curiously carved and rimmed; gravelled walks, and cool, delicious arbors starred with blossoms, invite the rich man and his wife to walk at sunset. The sunshine slants across the costly dwelling, and falls upon our humble home: the talk grows less; my boy, my prince puts up his blocks, and lays his books aside; 't is most time for papa; while Margaret climbs to the window ledge, and holding my baby high, we look and wait for the first step. Hush! he comes; the baby springs and gurgles; the sunshine falling on the rings of soft brown hair, her blue, laughing eyes lost in glee. This world holds not a lovelier face; and down the walk rings the gleeful shout, "Papa has come!" The baby is on his shoulder, with Jem and Margaret clinging to his hand.

Across the way, my neighbor looks and sighs; I know she 'd give it all to take my place, to lean as I do on this firm, strong arm, and romp with children up and down the walk.

The sun has gone to bed, and the children kneeling in their long white gowns, have made their little prayer. The white lids cover the laughing eyes, and the pink-tinged cheeks grow lovelier in repose. Priceless jewels! and sinking on my knees, I cannot but ask only more earnestly, that He will show me how to fashion and to polish them according to His will.

Withal, a genial home and parents' care is not enough to polish cornerstones. Other influences must be brought to bear; a wise correction and a mild rebuke. "Correct thy son and he shall give thee rest: yea, he shall give delight unto thy soul."

Mindful that look, word, and act are reflected truthfully, we are also to bear in mind that the occasions, the silent influences of our homes are educators. The taste of our children depends more upon the combination and arrangement of colors than we are usually aware. The plates in our picture-books, the figures on the wall, the pattern of the carpet, the hangings at the window, each has a part in moulding and forming: if not so, how do we account for preferences too strong for modern fashion to overcome? Said a gentleman, "I like to see a married lady, with a pretty, tasteful cap—I cannot remember when my mother did not wear one—and I cannot reconcile myself to a matron in plain hair, any more than I could to a young lady in her teens with her hair covered." Said another, "My mother always wore her dresses cut low, with a spencer or underhandkerchief, the prettiest fashion that a woman can wear, in my estimation."

Very few artists but go back to the time they hung about the mother, for the inspiration with which they have evoked beauty for a world to admire. If we question our own hearts, we shall no doubt find that taste was in a great measure formed before we left the nursery, proof positive of the permeating principle in a mother's influence. West tells us that it was the approbation of his mother that made him a painter. From time immemorial the encouragement of a mother has been a power to shape and fashion, little less than divine.

When our children grow out of our arms, like young birds just learning to fly, one of the most delightful places to lead them is into the garden and the meadow, with the birds, the bees, and the blossoms for companions; teaching them lessons of His love, showing them the flower-cups, and telling them by whose hand they were veined and painted, the spicy fragrance going up from the flowers in gratitude. The birds sing of His goodness, the bee murmurs his praise, and little children must love God.

"God makes them sing, mamma," says Margaret, hovering over the violet bed; "God makes Jem and me and baby sing; he 's a good God, mamma." And why not? Why must God be an abstract power? Why must heaven be so cold, so far off to our children? Not unless we choose to have it so. These little fluttering hearts are quick to learn who are our friends; they know the form and figure of the one we love best. If God is our Father, and Jesus is our dear Elder Brother, they will know it; and as they love us, so will they love those whom we love.

Not alone from the flower cups, the birds, the bees, and the blossoms, do we spell lessons suited to their capacity; but the tiny seeds we scatter, like the little words we plant in their hearts, take root, to bud and blossom after many days. There is no sham about nature, no pretence; her influences are pure, and her teaching is always elevating. True to herself, she fulfils all her promises; trusting her she does not betray that trust; the nearer we approach, the more we see in her to admire and to love. A precious privilege, to lead our loved ones through her arched galleries; to look upon their rapt faces, as for the first time they listen to the great organ chant in her mountain temple, drinking in the inspiration of her morning and evening hymns; their little hearts swelling with love, their sweet voices tuned to praise and thanksgiving. Pleasant to listen to the children's questions, while gathering flowers, and binding them with long feathery grass.

"God made 'em for us, mamma; He thought we 'd like 'em, maybe;" and clinging to my neck with her white, dimpled arms, my pearl, my "day's eye" talks of the heaven of which she has been told, the glittering gates and walls of jasper invisible; and still it seems so real to my child, that a sigh will come, unworthy and swept back. I would not have her love heaven less, nor grow to feel it farther off than she does now.

Another phase of truthfulness is accuracy, not a set form of speech, a studied manner, the sweet vivacity kept down with square and rule, but just the truth, giving the shade and measurement of another's speech. Children are more or less imaginative, fond of the marvellous, and liable to run wild, as roses in a wilderness of pink bloom. A judicious pruning, a gentle lopping off is required, if we would have a living, active, harmonious growth. A hero to himself, the boy's I's come in too quickly for knowledge to keep pace. A gentle training as we curl and twist the clambering vines, leading, not deadening, will throw the strength of brain into a strong aftergrowth.

The sun bridges the window with bars of gold; mirth is toned to a gentle seriousness; grasping her flowers, Margaret's blue eye turns homeward, and lifting my baby from the wealth of blossoms, I walk slowly. The sky bends over us in benediction, the earth sends up her vesper hymn, the air is full of love. Up the street stands the vine-wreathed cottage; the sunshine slants across the roof; my neighbor opposite is at the gate; the prancing bays clamp their silver bits.

A pretty turnout, but baby fails to see it; she has caught the trick from me, her papa says. No matter where, my baby is quick-eyed. "Ah, yes, 't is papa, papa," echoes Jem, as another figure approaches; and Margaret well nigh throws down her flowers in the blithe run to see which will be first to welcome him; while baby laughs and crows, and clasps her dimpled pink-tinged hands. We can afford to wait, our time will come—has come. My prince of men! not all my neighbor's wealth could make me feel as proud as I do now, with the great bronzed face so full of tenderness, looking into mine, the strong, firm hand on which to lean, the tender, loving voice, with questions of the day.

The gate is won, the burnished temple with the flower-wreathed door, and we the worshippers. "God is a good God, mamma." "A good God is our God," echoes through our hearts, and bending with our babes, we once more ask that truth and love may blend and work within us, making our lives fruitful in good deeds.

II.

"In Honor, Preferring One Another."

CHESTERFIELD has defined politeness to consist in benevolence in trifles; in other words, an unselfish interest in others. Looking into the mirror of God's word, we find, "As ye would that men should do to you, do ye also to them likewise; in honor, preferring one another." In no place or position is this rule more essential than in the family, and in no place, perhaps, is it more often neglected or ignored. It would seem the little kindly acts of daily life would be the natural outgrowth of the sacred bond that unites the household; yet there is, but too frequently, a certain boorishness that grows upon those connected by family ties, a strange forgetfulness of the little amenities of social life; allowing the manner to grow cold and rough, a scale of indifference under which the fire of love must burn brightly to be seen at all.

In most cases, no doubt this is done thoughtlessly; the husband taking it for granted that his wife has full confidence in his affection, unthinking that a fire never fed, must, as a matter of course, sooner or later go out. The wife, occupied with her duties as a wife and mother, grows unmindful of the morning courtesy and the evening welcome. So busy preparing something to eat and something to wear, that she is excusable perhaps; but then, was it a stranger going out and coming in, she would most assuredly have remembered that courtesy demands it; but it is her husband, and the good woman forgets that this may be the beginning of a breach through which the arrow will speed to her own heart.

It is often said that politeness costs nothing; and certainly in the family and out of it, it is a power to soften and do away with a thousand ills. The handclasp given to the stranger is but an act of politeness; the smile of recognition to the timid and the sorrowing is to be ascribed to the same benevolent principle: putting ourselves in the place of the stranger, and extending the same courtesy to him that we would wish extended to us.

Uniform politeness is one of the cornerstones in the Christian character; "doing as we would be done by;" "kindly affectioned one to another;" "courteous, given to hospitality:" "bear ye one another's burdens, and so fulfil the law of Christ." To be thus minded is not the work of the flesh, but of the Spirit; qualities not inherent to our sinful nature, but grafted on it through the influence of Divine teaching. As in every organization of imperfect beings forbearance and a kind consideration are needful, toning down prejudice, smoothing out the warp of preconceived opinion, blending and harmonizing temperaments and characters diverse and differently formed, so in the family a uniform politeness is necessary. It is the golden clasp in the chain of love, drawing the links closer and closer every day.

Looking into the mirror, we find, "Whatsoever things are lovely, whatsoever things are of good report," that do and teach. If politeness is needful in the family, we must practise it; if we desire to see our children courteous in their bearing to each other and to strangers, we must teach them to become so.

Said one lady to another, as they conversed in the drawing-room of a friend:

"I regret that I cannot send Annie to dancing-school. At home she has no one but her brothers to associate with, and boys are so rude."

"Do you think that going to such a school will have a tendency to rectify rudeness at home?" asked the lady.

"I should send her there to learn politeness, and then perhaps her brothers will not teaze her so dreadfully as they do now."

"If you feel that it is not best to send Annie this winter, I think I can furnish you with a code of politeness, the study of which would rectify rudeness in every instance," continued the lady.

"If you will be so good, it will greatly oblige me. Pray, where can I find it?"

"The only code of politeness that will produce radical effect on the home-life, is found in the Bible: the every-day practice of its teachings, with the uniform spirit it inculcates, will insure politeness in every place, and under whatever circumstances," was the answer.

Said another, "I consider myself fortunate in a nursery governess; she speaks French prettily, and her manners are quite Parisian."

I would not underrate speaking French prettily, neither would I object to the manners of nursery-maid and governess being refined and lady-like; but is this the chief requisite? Are there not intrinsic qualities that are to be looked for in those who assist us in the care and education of our children? Must we not feel a confidence that springs from qualities of heart and mind, formed after the teaching and the Spirit, under whose rule we wish our children to be taught? A parrot can be taught to speak French prettily, and a charlatan can bow as well as a gentleman; but for these accomplishments would we desire the worthless and unprincipled as the intimate associates of our children? Imitative in all their ways, they cannot live under the same roof without imbibing something of the same spirit as those with whom they dwell. If children associate with the good, the noble, and the true, they will almost uniformly become good, noble, and true; and in cases where they do not, may it not be traced to the effect of influence from a wrong and polluted source? an unseen spring, not the less deadly because hidden from the public gaze.

I have been surprised to note the conduct of my own children, the temptation through the influence of playmates to depart from accustomed usage. We were in the habit of entertaining an aged woman, and as the children had never seen either of their grandmothers, they were permitted to give her the endearing title. Seeing her at the gate one morning, I asked Jem to run down the walk to meet her. It had always been his custom, without my suggestion, but this time he delayed.

"Run, my child."

"Pshaw, it 's only grandma. Let her come in by herself."

Surprised, as I had never heard him speak in this manner, my look revealed it. The small face was troubled, and he drew near me.

"She knows the way, if she can't see very well," and the voice grew tender.

"She may know the way, but it would

please her. If papa was here, he would go."

"But, mamma," and the child hesitated, while the tears sprang into his brown eyes, "Stephen says it is all nonsense to be polite to people you see every day."

"People that we see every day are just the ones to whom we should be kind and attentive; and to be kind and attentive is to be polite."

"He says it takes too much time to run and open the door for everybody; and the next time grandma drops her handkerchief, let her pick it up."

"Grandma cannot see as well as she could once; she trembles, and her hand shakes. It troubles her to stoop, and she is tired all the time. My little boy is strong; he can eat and sleep, can see, and hear, and run; still, he is not willing to be courteous. Who will wait upon him, should he live to be old?"

The tears were running down Jem's cheeks; he put up his hand to wipe them away, and then pressed his face still nearer to mine.

"Mamma, will Jesus know?"

"Jesus knows now, and he is grieved. Much as mamma loves Jem, Jesus loves him still more."

"O mamma, I do n't want him to know;" and the small arms were clinging to my neck. "I wish he would n't look at me just now. Is it written down, mamma?"

"I fear it is."

"O mamma, I can't have it, I can't have it;" and the child's heart was stirred to its inmost depths.

"If my boy is really sorry, and will try to remember, Jesus will rub it out."

"What will he do with it? Do ask him, mamma; I can't have it there."

"Jesus loved Jem, and he shed his

blood that the black stain of sin might be washed white. If we ask, he will do it."

"He wont hear me now, I know. Do ask him, please; I can't have it there. He loves you, mamma."

"My asking will not do for my little boy; he must himself ask."

"Go with me, mamma, please. I've been so bad he wont look at me; but if he knows I'm your little boy, and that I'm real sorry, he'll rub it out; I want to see him do it." And kneeling before the throne of grace we asked that this sin might be blotted out; that in the future we might be enabled to carry out the injunction, "In honor, preferring one another," studying each other's comfort, remembering especially the deference due to the aged, the infirm, and humble disciple. "Inasmuch as ye have done it unto one of the least of these, ye have done it unto me."

Looking into this mirror, we find that constant care and watchfulness is required. "Be not deceived; evil communications corrupt good manners;" "for what fellowship hath righteousness with unrighteousness, and what communion hath light with darkness?" If we desire to see our children pure, we must be careful that their associations are pure, the friendships they make, the books they read, the thoughts they cherish. Every day ideas are awakened, and impressions made. What shall they be, is a question that seems ever sounding through the inmost chambers of the mother's heart. What ideas? what impressions? Is it the privilege of the mother to take the place of photographer, or can she delegate it to another?

The artist, painting for all time; the sculptor, moulding for eternity, does not look upon his work as drudgery. It is his lifework; his heart goes out, every stroke of the brush; every fall of the hammer reveals in a measure the beauty that he sees and feels. The four sides of his studio expand; he sees in fancy an immense gallery filled with works of art: a long roll of names, and among them he sees his own. His work is unveiled; silent and still the crowds pause to admire; his ear is greeted with words of commendation and praise; tears are in his eyes; he weeps, but they are tears of joy; the little studio and the days of incessant toil are forgotten. List! the plaudit, "Well done!" It is music to his heart, it well repays him for all the sacrifice.

Is not the mother this painter, tracing figures for all time? Is she not this sculptor, moulding and fashioning a soul for eternity? Glorious work! on earth there is nothing to equal it; angels have nothing more praiseworthy. This little mystic life, that caught its throbbing from her own heart, and to which her soul is indissolubly united, can be polished by her more readily than by another; it is her lifework. Like one of old, she "cannot come down." Far away she sees a palace, fairer and more beautiful than mortal eyes have ever seen; her work is to shine there. She sees the white robes, the crowns, the harps; and there is one for her, there is one for each of her babes. The long, weary days are forgotten, the watchful care, the tedious lessons often repeated and long time in being learned, are not regretted. Up to these magnificent courts she sees the way. The Judge is there; she longs to look upon his face, she longs to kneel before him; "Behold, I and the children whom the Lord hath given me."

While it is given the mother in an

especial sense, to form and polish, the duty is not so exclusively hers that it cannot be performed by another. Indeed, it is often done by those who are no manner of kin; the only bond requisite is a heart brimming over with love, anxious to work for Christ, and seeing in every child, however destitute, the germ of a life that may be trained for usefulness here and happiness hereafter.

A bereaved mother may be won to love and adopt for her own some sweet-faced orphan child who she fancies looks like her own lost darling, and on whom she is willing to lavish all a mother's love and affection.

My neighbor over the way no longer looks and sighs. A sweet, fair face, with laughing blue eyes, and long, soft curls of sunny hair, sits beside her. Gertrude is very lovely. My neighbor looks and smiles. It happened thus:

The venerable woman, of whom mention has been made, lived with a grandchild up four flights of stairs. One day she grew too weary to come down the tedious length, and the next, God saw how faint and weak she was; and moved by love for her and for the child, he sent an angel to take her up still higher. Her sands were almost run. The tongue had well-nigh lost its power; but it was enough for my husband and me to know the woman's wish, that henceforth Gertrude should be to us as Margaret.

The winter proved a hard one for the poor. It was well, we said, that grandma went to sleep before the cold came on; and Gertrude, curling up into a ball before the cheerful fire, played making books with pictures in them, to suit the taste of baby Maude. It was autumn when Gertrude came to play with baby Maude; the flowers were well-nigh gone, the brown earth sere and chill, good fires were needful. My neighbor's house was closed; I did not see her leave, but I knew the very hour. There was a dull, cold look outside; we should miss her just as one would miss a costly painting on the wall, a statue fallen from its place.

The spring came round, and when the long June days warmed up the earth, and wove rich beauty from every nook and dell, my neighbor reappeared. The baby crowed and laughed, and Gertrude clapped her hands. It was a pretty sight; the pale, sad face lighting up with smiles as she saw baby, turning her eyes half drowned in tears, as she caught the name "Gertrude."

A quick thought flashed through my brain; this woman had been a mother. I saw it, felt it, realized the kinship for the first time; strange that I had been so dull. Catching her eye in the fulness of my joy, I held my baby up, her silvery glee and laughter-loving eyes sending a pang to my neighbor's heart. Ah, me! she too, had known the joy of motherhood. A mother's loss and sorrow had been hers, I saw it now. A little fleeting life, and I was sure the angels knew the child, and called away her Gertrude.

Days passed. I saw the mother's face grow pale and thin; her step was slow, and her head bowed as all too heavy for the slender neck. What right had I to so much happiness? How could I sit and drink my fill, without a drop to quench my neighbor's thirst? My husband knew my thought, and his great heart, while tender, swerved not from the right.

"If she will love her for her own, and bring her up to be a good, true woman; but if not, she shall not have her. I will not risk her soul for all the benefit of added wealth."

I knew that he was right, he always is; and making sure of all that I could learn, I dressed Gertrude in her prettiest frock, and curling her sunny hair over my finger, bound it back with a blue ribbon, leaving her forehead white and pure. A dainty pair of gaiters Margaret had, and into these I slid the well-shaped foot, and taking Gertrude by the hand, we crossed the street, and through my neighbor's gate. She met me graciously; the sweet, pale lady took my hand in hers, and asked me, as a sister would have done, the health of all at home. Then, looking down, she kissed the upturned face of the sweet child.

"And this is Gertrude? I have heard her name. We had a Gertrude once, and I have fancied—"

The voice was gone. I slid my arm

around the lady's waist, and kissed her on the lips. She kissed me back, and I, forgetful that her dress was silk, and mine of common stuff, whispered of Gertrude, and that the winter had been stern to us poor folk.

"Give her to me, and know that I will love her as my own. Henceforth she shall be to me as my own lost Gertrude. But stop." And unwinding her arms that had been clasped around me, she flew down the walk to a small arbor covered with pink bloom. Lifting her snowy hand she swept back the fragrant curtain, and the next we saw she stood leaning on the arm of a gray-haired man, the tears, like two great pearls, still glistening, but her face bright and radiant with love.

"My child, my Gertrude, will you stay with us, and may we love and care for you as our very own?" while the proud man lifted the little trembler in his arms, and kissed her as a father would have done. My eyes were full; I turned a look to our small home; she will be happier here, if they will love her, and bring her up to fear and love the Lord.

The lady read my thought, and sweetly said:

"We are unworthy followers of the same Lord; unworthy, most unworthy, grasping, with outstretched hand, his many gifts; but when he sent a messenger to take the one most loved and latest given, we murmured; and for this he sent leanness into our souls, leaving us to sit in darkness, until we came to a better mind." Then drawing close, she kissed me again, and told me of the lesson she had learned, and how she hoped never to grow forgetful of His love.

We missed Gertrude for a time, and

Jem and Margaret were lost in their little plays without her; but we knew that it would be better for her in the future; a broader culture she would have, perhaps, with added means for usefulness and doing lasting good.

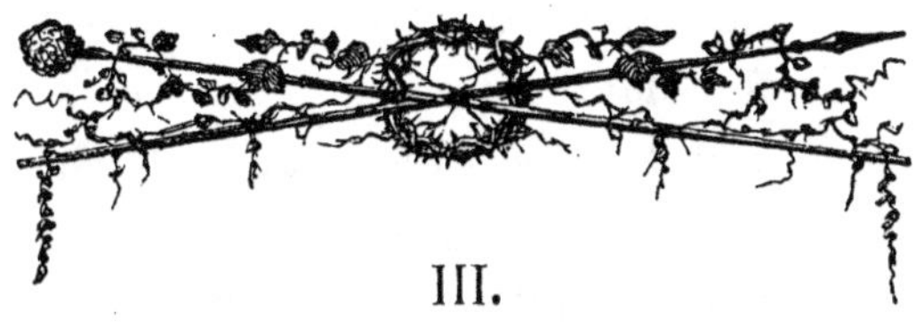

III.

The Fear of Ridicule.

AMONG the various motives that influence us for good or for evil, none is more universal or more powerful in its effects than the fear of ridicule. Deep down in the nature of every created being is an honest desire to be approved by friends and associates, and the knowledge of their displeasure, even with natures the most independent, rarely fails to give pain. But the pang that arises from the want of approval is nothing, to the sting caused by the sarcastic smile, the covert shaft of ridicule.

Especially to the young, who are the

most keenly alive to its influence, is its power often fatal. Watching the children, I have learned to look at it as one of the greatest enemies that, as mothers, we have to contend with. It affords so natural, easy, and insidious an excuse for dereliction in duty. Much of the exaggeration, equivocation, and falsehood in our children has its origin in this source. It is an inherent evil, that can only be overcome by cultivating firmness, stability, and courage. Careful to implant right principles and correct views in the hearts of our children, we must also teach them to prize a higher standard of excellence than mere human opinion; regarding their own self-respect, pure motives, and conscious integrity, as foundation stones on which the future manhood and womanhood is to be built.

I am aware that many will say that a

subject of this nature is altogether too grave to refer to in the presence of young children. I admit that, should we thrust it upon our children without due care of mental strength and capacity, it would probably do little good. More, it would do positive harm; for what overloads the child's mind, like the food that overloads his stomach, weakens rather than tends to strength. Milk belongs to babes; but as our children grow in years there is not much danger in giving them meat occasionally; pap does not tend to strength and activity. True, we are to chop it fine, and to insist on its being well masticated; and the effect we see in the bright, healthy countenances usually seen in children that are well fed, and have plenty of air and sunshine.

Especially is it in childhood that all needful lessons are to be given by the mother; for as they grow in years, they grow in a sense away from us; that is, other influences creep in, weakening the effect of our words by the wider range of unexplored territory it is now theirs to tread. If, through fear of ridicule, they cannot say "No" to the enticements of their associates, there is little hope that they will be able in after years to maintain their integrity against the assaults of the adversary, always ready to seize upon the ignorant and the unwary. Many a youth open to good influences, has been sunk to the level of the worthless and vicious, by the dread of their sneer and the fear of their contempt. Many a young man, ignorant of the world and weak in principle, has been urged on by degrees to sacrifice his integrity, to sully his manhood, and to steep his whole nature in the black pool of sin, simply because he could not brave the laugh of his companions. Many a daughter has turned to the grave as the only place to hide her shame, because she had not strength of principle sufficient to say "No" when asked to ride on the Sabbath, to go to the theatre, or to some objectionable place of amusement.

If we would insure our sons and our daughters from such a fate, we must teach them the true end and aim of life from their infancy. Living in an age like ours, there is double danger lest the true scale of excellence be reversed, placing the body above the mind, and the mind above the heart; our sons priding themselves in strength and activity, wit, and geniality, in the room of strict integrity and high moral principle; our daughters on personal beauty, light, graceful accomplishments, and a winning fluency of speech, in the room of purity and a firm and abiding Christian faith, the only safeguard for a woman.

The fear of ridicule, while it is keenly felt by children and youth, does not exclusively belong to them. It is very possible, that as mothers, we are still under its baneful influence; doing as others do, dressing as others dress, merging our own individual acts and opinions into those of our neighbor; craving sympathy from broken reeds and empty pitchers, in the room of leaning with heart and soul upon the sure foundation that is given us in the gospel. Woman, as being the more sensitive, is certainly the most subject to the fear of ridicule. Hence, she requires a more unwearied diligence, lest this fear betray her into covert or open neglect of known duty. The more sensitive the nature, the more liable to be in bondage to this fear. Many a student has not been proof against the laugh of the most indolent scholar in his class: "There goes the plodder," or the son of a poor man working his way up by the labor of his hands, ready to yield the point, throw aside his books, and sit down in despair, because some idle spendthrift taunted him with his necessity. Industry will overcome poverty; perseverance and indomitable energy are more to the student than mere natural gifts, or talents without application.

To say "No," is as needful for the child as it is for the man. The first great requisite demanded by a wise and judicious parent is obedience. Children are subject to temptation quite as much as youth and middle age; small paths, it is true, but in the direction of error just the same. To abstain from wrong-doing as a child requires principle; not the principle of a man, but of a child. This principle is not the natural product of the heart, it is implanted there to be nourished, strengthened, fed by a mother's care and devotion. The mother's duty in this particular is not unlike the gardener's; he begins to train his vines when they are young and tender; he turns and twists them, he inclines them to twine about the support he offers; he does not allow them to choose for themselves; the growth is theirs, but the manner depends upon him. He does more; he obliges them, making them fast, and laying weights upon them, until time has made it natural for them to take that direction. Should the gardener leave his vines for a season, what a mass! tangled, confused, unsightly. His first care is to cut down, clip, and confine the young growth. True, with vigorous means he may bring back beauty and order, but it will require double work;

and with this it will of necessity require time before harmony will be established.

With an exceedingly sensitive nature, affectionate, and still under fear of ridicule from his associates, Jem has taught me many a lesson that I should not have learned without him. Willing to give him a little pleasure, his father had taken him to spend a few days with a friend who had a large family of children, most of them boys. For lodging room the boys slept in the same apartment, small cots standing in rows. Jem was honored with one of these quite by himself, the first night. Taking advantage of the occasion when the boys stood with their backs to him, Jem kneeled as he had been accustomed to do, said his prayer hurriedly, and slipped into bed, unobserved as he thought, by every eye.

The next night, there was the addition of another visitor, a boy larger and more advanced in knowledge; and this boy was given to share Jem's bed. It now required more courage to do his duty, and for a long time, as he afterwards told me, he deliberated. "If I kneel," he argued, "Richard is so full of fun he will be sure to see me, and will call the attention of the other boys and they will laugh at me. I cannot endure it." Conscience was faithful, however; it had always been his custom not to close his eyes in sleep before he had gone to God in prayer. He realized that it was right; he felt that he could not sleep without it, and still he could not do so without the risk of being laughed at by his associates. At length his duty was too plain for him to refuse; he must kneel and pray silently.

"Softly! softly! I thought he was a Methodist," and Richard crept up behind him and pulled his hair till he cried out.

"Ha, ha, all pretence—was praying a minute ago," and a boyish laugh echoed through the room.

A trying place I see, my son, and must have taxed your patience; but prayer is the breathing of the heart's desire to God, and whatever the posture of the body, should not be omitted as we retire to rest. All the world over there will be those to scorn and deride you in your attempts to serve God; but knowing the evil, we must not be overcome by it, our trust must be in him. As a little boy you need to ask him to keep you from doing wrong, and should you live to become a man, you will have the same need to ask him. In the world, my child, we cannot live without God.

Temptations to evade duty are not confined to children. I may be allowed to mention an incident in the life of a lady well known in the religious and literary world. In early life this lady had the misfortune to lose her father, and with him the wealth by which he had been enabled to surround his family with all the luxuries and refinements of life. Delicate in health, a child but just entering her teens, she was educated beyond her years, with a look and manner that spoke maturity of thought and purpose. A proficient in music, and anxious to make her education available for her mother and little brothers, she asked and obtained a position as music teacher in a female seminary in an adjoining state. She had not been engaged in teaching more than six months before cholera broke out in the vicinity, and the principal of the seminary, a clergyman advanced in years and exceedingly delicate, fell by it.

At once the school was in alarm.

There was dread in the very name. Letters were written and trunks packed; the English teachers, older by a decade of years, had no power to pacify their pupils. Not another case was fatal; and still, if the rumor got afloat, the school would be broken up.

In this emergency the young music teacher called the roll and explained the nature of the disease, and the cause of the principal's death. She next demanded the letters, ordered the trunks to be unpacked, and assured them that there was no ground for special alarm, and that the school in all its appointments would go on as usual. Order was restored, and confidence established.

The wife of the clergyman, overcome with grief at the loss of her husband, and inefficient to manage for herself, had looked upon it as a settled thing that the school must be broken up; but with the reaction it was surprising to see how she leaned upon the self-appointed principal. Not only the school, but the domestic department was under her supervision. Morning and evening devotion, as well as chapel duties devolved upon this young lady. Timid and shrinking, it was upon ordinary occasions a cross; while the addition of guests made it still more keenly felt.

One evening as the weary girl watched the day go out, a carriage entered the yard, and she caught a glimpse of an elegant-looking elderly man, his wife, and as she judged two daughters. Every thing about them showed culture and refinement. Introductions were made. It was Judge W—— and family, a man of acknowledged worth and distinction, the brother of the widowed woman in whose name the school was conducted.

The evening passed. At nine o'clock, through the ample halls the bell sounded for family prayers; the teacher had not thought of it, but with the first stroke of the bell it came unbidden: What if the guests should be there? What if the learned judge should refuse to lead? The notes of the bell died away, the last footfall was heard on the stairs. A moment and the teacher crossed the hall to the parlor. The pupils, the family, and the guests were seated. In the centre of the room stood a small table, with a chair beside it, and on it lay a Bible and hymn-book. With a graceful bow the teacher turned to the judge and politely asked him to occupy the chair. The invitation was refused.

"What was I to do?" said the teacher, as years afterwards she related the incident. "If I faltered, it would bring reproach upon the name of Jesus. To go forward seemed impossible. My head reeled, and my hands trembled visibly.

"Turning to the hundred and third Psalm, I read. Before I had reached the line, 'Like as a father pitieth his children, so the Lord pitieth them that fear him. For he knoweth our frame, he remembereth that we are dust,' I was calm. It was our habit to sing after reading; and striking into a familiar hymn, I noticed that the judge was greatly moved, and before its close he arose and left the room. The visitors remained several days; but at prayer morning and night there was no more trepidation.

"The morning he left," continued the lady, "after our usual service, the judge followed in prayer. It was a sweet simple petition, and caused us ever after to remember him as a personal friend. As he rose from his knees he came to me, the tears rolling down his manly cheeks, and taking my hand thanked me for the lesson he had learned. 'I have been a member of the church for years; but so much am I absent from home that I have allowed myself to omit family prayer. I am going home now to revive it, and I thank you for not hesitating in your duty; my wife and daughters bless you for the example given them.'

"Words are weak to describe my own feelings. I had hesitated, trembled, and almost fallen. I can never be sufficiently thankful that God sustained me. Had I then denied him, my whole after life perhaps would have been changed."

Thus it is, there are turning points, decisions to be made by children and youth as well as by people of mature years. Training children, we cannot exempt them from temptation. There are foes within and foes without; but we must teach them to stand firm in their integrity, to make the love of God their guide, to remember that the eye of Jehovah is upon them, and that there is nothing for them to fear if they go forward in the discharge of all known duty.

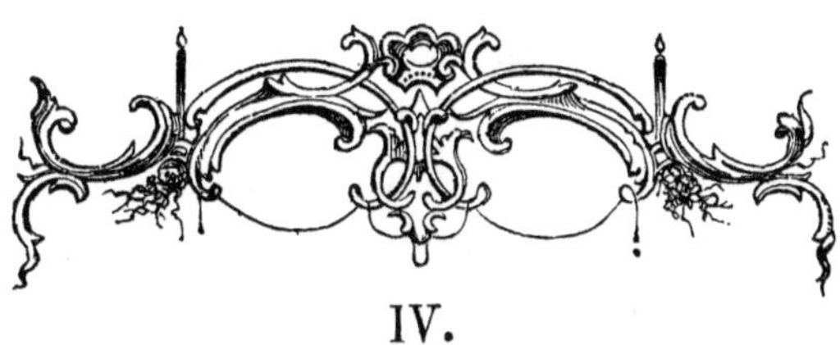

IV.

Home Duties.

LIFE is made up of littles, and home duties are the aggregate of littles, difficult to enumerate, but easily performed; a nameless grace and beauty wrapping in the habitation, let it be a lordly palace or a settler's hut. Home is where the mother is, the mother's care and counsel investing it with a sanctity not to be found elsewhere. Poets have sung, and orators have loved to dwell upon the theme; but poets and orators, in their grandest achievements, fail to equal the pictures enshrined in each heart. Language is weak to portray the emotion as we visit the old home; the same old hall, with the substantial oak staircase, and the tall old-fashioned clock on the landing. Years are forgotten; only yesterday, and we were children dancing through the room. The furniture is not the same, the paper on the wall is modern in its style; but to us the well-remembered faces, the chair in which a mother sat, the broad staircase, and the window in the angle of the wall, have a strange significancy.

A blithe set of romping girls and boys, our mirth softened to cheerfulness as we gathered round this same old chair. Margaret, my Margaret, wears our mother's name, and in my turn do I try to teach my child in keeping with her rule.

It is pleasant to watch the fair child's face, the light of intelligence breaking over it, the budding thought, the wealth of feeling, the awakening imagination, the kindling fancy: pleasant inasmuch as it charms with its beauty, its freshness, its sweet hopefulness, a charming seriousness creeping up as I look. This fair child, with her richly freighted mind and heart, is mine to polish for a "cornerstone," around which other foundations will be laid, a temple beautiful and fair to look upon. How shall I order it?

In the mirror of God's word we find an admirable picture of home life: "Her children arise up and call her blessed, her husband also and he praiseth her;" again, "Let them learn first to show piety at home," "not slanderers; sober, faithful in all things."

By this it would seem that piety is the first requisite. Coveting, first of all, "the best gifts," "the one thing needful;" knowing that all requisite good will be added.

I have sometimes been afraid that much of the preciousness connected with our duties as mothers escapes us through our failure to become acquainted with the temperament and condition of our children. Much of the effectiveness of our Saviour's teaching when upon earth arose from the fact that "He knew what was in man," tempering his speech to suit the necessity of the case. To the mother this personal knowledge is all-important: tracing back, as she is able to do, the phases in her own life, the impressions and influences distinctly brought to mind in the habits and inclinations of her children. This is one of the chief reasons why the work of training so exclusively belongs to the mother, the more intimate knowledge that she possesses bringing her more in sympathy with the nature of her child, and enabling her to prove a skilful workman in shaping and polishing the life committed to her care.

In doing this there can be no precise form of speech or manner; neither can any formula of rules be strictly adhered to. Of the children of the same mother no two are exactly alike: the same form of speech calculated to praise or to reprove one would not be judicious when used for another. In the same disease the physician seldom treats two cases precisely alike. As a physician, the first care is to understand as much as it is possible for him to know, of the temperament, constitution, and habits of his patient. Then he notes the disease and makes out his diagnosis. This is the reason that we place so much confidence in the family physician: he is acquainted with our constitution, he knows what the system can bear, he is acquainted with the constitution of each of our children, which gives us a confidence in his treatment, that we could not feel in a stranger.

The eye of the patient reveals much to the physician; the brow, the cheek, the lip are all interpreters. He lays his finger on the telltale pulse, he puts himself in sympathy with his patient, his whole being is absorbed in his work, the life of his patient is in his hands, it will be required of him. A trifling neglect, or an ill-made figure, a false weight, or imperfect measurement, and the life is lost. The physician knows this, and he watches and notes every change. He dares not delegate it to another; however weary he may be, he is not satisfied until he has made his round.

All this is done by the conscientious physician to save a temporal life. Eternal life is the care of the mother. Can she prove less watchful? Can she with more security neglect her duty? Can she suffer herself to make a mistake?

In view of such responsibility, what mother would but tremble in accepting the charge were it not for the promises: "Lo, I am with you alway;" "All things whatsoever ye shall ask in prayer, believing, ye shall receive;" "Ask and it shall be given you;" "If any of you lack wisdom let him ask of God, and it shall be given him." The Scriptures distinctly teach that home is the legitimate realm of woman, the ordering of her household and the training of her children her highest duty, her sweetest privilege. In the fulfilment of this duty, honor has always awaited her, "her own works praise her in the gates."

Premising that, as mothers feeling the weight of individual responsibility we are to consult the mirror of God's word, we will consider more particularly home duties, and the necessity laid upon us to render home the most attractive place that can be found by our children. This does not of necessity require wealth, or extravagance in outfit. A mother's arms in fond endearment, are more that frescoed walls and elegant hangings. The humblest room is beautified by her smile, the most magnificent one will be cold and barren without it. Many a child and many a youth goes astray, not because his home is not well appointed, but simply because home lacks sunshine. Many, through over zeal to be called good housekeepers, disgust and repel, without seeming to be conscious where the mistake lies. A fly lighting on the wall has power to disturb them. A beam of sunshine quite throws them into a fever. To be neat and orderly is praiseworthy, but to shut out the light and sunshine for fear that the furniture will be injured, or the carpet faded, is like throwing away pearls and gathering pebbles.

Children live in the present, they are fond of brightness, they love the sunshine, and it is natural for them to seek the place where they find it. If home is the spot where every thing is dark and gloomy, with sour faces, harsh words and continual fault-finding, rest assured they will spend as little time as possible there. On the contrary, if father and mother unite to make it beautiful, the father expending according to his means, giving his children to see that he desires their happiness, and is doing all that he can to insure it; the mother, lighthearted, happy, winsome, remembering her own youth, enjoying a good healthful romp with her children, showing her interest by talking with and entertaining them as she does her friends, entering into the spirit of their games, reading, studying, putting herself in sympathy with them, the probabilities are that such a mother will never be called to mourn the downfall of a son or a daughter.

A bright cheerful home is a place of security in times of temptation and danger. Blessed the remembrance of such a home: the walls plain and unassuming, furniture simple, books and pictures few but admirably arranged, while over all is the genial loving smile of the mother, the warm hand-clasp, the kiss. Humble as their home is, the children will never find another to equal it. Such homes are foretastes of the final home with our dear heavenly Father. It will be all sunshine there, all love, all happiness.

Another effectual way to render home happy to our children, is to give them something to do. It awakens their interest and deepens their love; they are led to look upon themselves as in a sense essential to their parents; it kindles a desire to please, and thus invested with a share of responsibility there is a certain child dignity to be supported, an unconscious deepening of principles. Some years since, on a visit to a friend whose little son, a bright manly boy of eight summers, was particularly winning, I was impressed with the benefits to be derived from this course. On being asked to return with me and spend a few days, his reply was, "My father cannot spare me;" his whole appearance showing how much he valued the idea of being useful to his father; heightening his own self-respect, and having a tendency to render him more manly.

Children are naturally helpful; their daily activities can be turned into profitable channels, or allowed to run to waste, according to the mother's influence. It is a sad thing to see a child bowed down under burdens too heavy for it; but if we would have our children happy, we must let them bear the yoke in their youth; giving them certain duties and holding them responsible for the fulfilment of those duties.

Of necessity these should be light, not given as a tax, but as a duty, the performance intended to bring pleasure. Duties thus performed will give them a relish for work in after life, and custom will render it easy. In my own case, the first duty given to Margaret was to dust papa's study chair. This was to be done every morning at a specified time. Jem was taught to bring his father's dressing gown and slippers as he came in at night. This was not exacted of him merely as something to be done; but to stimulate his memory and render him mindful of such little acts of courtesy, esteeming it a greater favor to assist others than to be assisted by them.

As they grew older more was required of them, not enough to weary, but sufficient to give zest to recreation; they were not less active at their games, while they grasped study with a firmer hold, a more abiding love. In gardening they were permitted to have a share, a certain pride in possession showing itself on their faces and in their words. Each was provided with a set of small tools, always to be put in their respective places when they had been used. In this manner, health was won and the whole mental machinery gained strength. Nature is a wonderful teacher: not even a child can come in contact with her without visible improvement.

Stronger by degrees the mind grows as the body strengthens, and many a lesson of trust and patient waiting was learned in the garden. Precious little helpers! How they soften the cares and the burdens of life. Calm, confident, and trusting in our knowledge and judgment, what a lesson do they teach us of security in the guardianship of our dear heavenly Father. Many times, when my soul was troubled and heavy with care, have I looked into the calm bright faces around me. "You can make it all right, mamma," were words that rung through my heart-chambers. Such love and confidence my children had in me: while I, knowing that a Father's love was mine, that a precious Elder Brother was touched with my infirmities, was yet often weak and desponding.

Gertrude not unfrequently joined us in our work, bringing in her hand a rare flower, a climbing rose, or a vine: something to be to us a remembrancer.

Each day increased her beauty—a precious bud unfolding where all was fair; a blessing in her new home, the gentle childlike air and manner winning more than her words.

"Mamma," exclaimed Margaret, as her hour in the garden expired, and she turned to her lessons, "I love the garden better than any of my books."

"Do you call the garden a book?"

"You know what you have often told me, that every leaf was a letter; and I thought if the leaves were letters, the whole world would make a book."

"True, in that case it is a book written with the finger of God, each leaf a letter from which we are to spell lessons of love, of joy and thankfulness."

Who that listens to the child's query, that stops to analyze child-feeling, or attempts to answer a twentieth of the questions asked, can for a moment think that there is a period in their lives when the highest intellectual gifts are not called into requisition? Milk is diluted to give to babes, and meat is given in dainty morsels. It is not in quantity, but in quality the same as the man of full grown power requires. Thus with instruction, it should be the best, the choicest, the most attractive, served up to suit the strength of the mental palate, inclining the child to desire more.

The Bible is replete with evidence that childhood is the time to make an intelligent choice of God's service. From the beginning when the Creator instituted the family relation, down to the time when the Saviour enjoined it upon Peter to prove his love by caring for the lambs, lawgivers, prophets, priests, and apostles have taught that children are the especial charge of our heavenly Father, to be received and loved and instructed as those who could best understand, and most readily believe in and serve Him. "Except ye be converted and become as little children, ye shall not enter into the kingdom of heaven." "Whosoever shall not receive the kingdom of God as a little child, shall in no wise enter therein." Who so ready to be taught as a child? Who so ready to believe, so frank, so confiding? Such love is very precious in the sight of God. The fragrance of the opening bud is deeper than that of the full blown flower. Home duties are precious in proportion as they are blended with love to God: his glory being of paramount importance; his love filling our hearts and the hearts of our children with peace.

In connection with this, I remember to have heard a mother say she feared that if her children were taught to breathe in the atmosphere of God's love, thinking and acting and living as in his presence, they would fail to know by experience the regenerating influence of his Spirit in their hearts.

"Only believe," is the requirement. Belief is the foundation of the Christian faith. What have brain power and years of mental training to do with this? "The wisdom of the world is foolishness with God." There is no fitness attained through knowledge or learning, no virtue in waiting a specified term of years. "With the heart man believeth unto righteousness." The undoubting clinging trust of the child is the one thing needful: "Now is the accepted time; behold, now is the day of salvation." Was it not in view of this truth that Jesus said, "I thank thee, O Father, Lord of heaven and earth, because thou hast hid these things from the wise and prudent, and hast revealed them unto babes."

Not too young! Oh no, not too young! My heart thrills with rapture as I look into Margaret's upturned face, lay my hand on Jem's brown head, and draw Maude, my dove-eyed Maude, to my bosom. Not too young to come to Jesus. Dear ones! may I not as a mother fail to plant the seeds of truth in your hearts from fear that the soil is not old enough to receive it!

In mimic play children imitate those of larger growth: their doll-gatherings and tea-parties are on the same plan as those they have been accustomed to see the mother serve; they try to do and to say exactly what they understand to be in keeping with the occasion: receiving and entertaining their guests with a strange blending of child grace and womanly dignity that would be ridiculous if not for its ingenuousness.

I was forcibly impressed with this

during a few days' serious illness. It was a a season when it was almost impossible to secure a nurse. In this dilemma, Margaret was our little nurse and housekeeper. Too ill to give directions, I was surprised to see how closely the child imitated her mother's movements: a certain order pervaded the room; and while she brought the medicine, dropped it into a spoon, and made nourishing drinks for me, she also set the table and prepared the meals for the family.

"Do not think about it, mamma, it will make your head ache; papa says that I do very nicely." Sweet lesson of patient doing; and lying with closed eyes, I tried to take it in: the simple child-faith, never once murmuring that she did not know more, was not older, and of course more able; but thankful and willing to do her best, feeling approved of her own conscience, and well pleased with the commendation of her parents. At breakfast and tea, the small housewife perched herself in mamma's chair, giving papa his cup, a touching gravity on the young fair face, that rendered it only the more attractive.

It is a mistaken idea that helpfulness tends to a stiff mature manner, repulsive as shown in a child. To be helpful does not crush out the glee and playfulness of the child nature. On the contrary, their young hearts bubble over with more freshness. A bow that is always bent, loses its vigor, and continual play ceases to have a charm even for a child.

As much of the happiness of home depends upon the dignity and ease with which the nameless daily duties are discharged, it becomes us as mothers to invest the most menial service with an air of cheerfulness, never considering it a reproach to be found superintending or doing with our own hands whatever tends to the completeness of a well-ordered household. It is too much the custom to cry out against the petty exactions, the confinement and care necessary to the mistress of a family; making mountains out of mole-hills; driven, nettled, throwing aside responsibility if possible; breaking up, boarding, or leaving all to servants, regarding even the care of their own children as too much labor and trouble. Let this habit prevail, and what security have we that our sons will ripen into honorable manhood? that our daughters will rise up and call us blessed?

If we would reap, we must first plant the seed. Neither can this be done without a careful preparation. There is no chance work: there is an end and an aim. Neglect our duties we may, delegate them to others, or leave them to the mercy of circumstances; but responsibility will still cling to us, and at last the account must be rendered, and the reward will be proportioned to our faithfulness.

V.

What Shall We Read?

IN this age of books, newspapers, and magazines, this question is one of vital importance. What shall we read? What shall our children read? There are now so many really good books, especially for the young, that it involves judgment and taste, as well as principle, to make a judicious choice. In adorning a temple, the workman chooses, out of the abundance of gold and silver and precious stones, such as fit the purpose and the end in view. Those that he rejects may be as valuable as any, but not so well adapted to his present need.

To read all the good books would be an impossibility, even if we had the means to obtain them. To read without a prescribed course would be no better for the intellect, than food would be for the body when taken at all hours, regardless of the stomach and the work it has to do in digestion.

"I never saw such a thirst for reading as my son has," said one lady to another; "it is nothing but read, read. We can hardly get him to take necessary exercise."

"Ah," returned the lady, "to be a diligent reader is certainly commendable. What kind of reading does your son prefer?"

"Oh, any thing. He just reads all the time."

The mother spoke with the tone of one who felt that her son was to be commended. The lady was surprised, and upon a fitting occasion questioned the son. Alas! he did read all the time, as his mother said, the sickly sensational stories brought to him through the columes of his favorite newspapers; feeding on husks, worse than husks, light, foamy, evanescent. No; they left a stain on the soul, a taste in the mouth, that will effectually deprive him of a relish for any thing better. What mother would not cry out to see her son feeding on garbage, seeking it through the gutters? And is there a mother that can see her child devouring poison, forgetful of present duty, lost in the dreams of the novelist, and not cry out against it?

As mothers, cannot we teach our children to cultivate a purer taste, to shun as they would the plague the pictures of vice and demoralization? Cannot we teach them to abstain from impure literature, just as we teach them not to tamper with opium, with alcohol and tobacco? It will not do to hesitate. The evil is abroad. We must meet it; not with a captious, fault-finding spirit, but lovingly, holding up the mirror of God's word, drawing just inferences and conclusions, constrained by its teaching rather than our own to see that it is impossible for the mind to dwell on scenes such as are represented in too many of our books and papers, without receiving impressions injurious to the progress of positive good in the soul.

It will not be sufficient to show them the baneful effects of such reading, but we must teach them what to read, choosing for them, and cultivating taste as well as higher mental faculties, and leading them to choose wisely for themselves. Cannot we teach our children that the daily study of God's word is indispensable? Fond of stories, romantic and imaginative, what book so well calculated to charm them by the variety of its themes, the interest of its history, the matchless beauty of its poetry, the depth of its science, the simplicity and power of its oratory? So varied is it, and so enlarged in its scope, that were there not another book within his reach, the thorough Bible-student would be justly considered a learned man.

To impress our children with the beauty and interest of the Bible, we must feel them ourselves. In order to inculcate its truths, we must honor them in our lives: to win daily study, we must ourselves daily study the Scriptures, we must speak of them and consult them, making them the rule and the standard of daily life. To win our children to love what we love, we must bring before their understanding the truth which tends to excite or call forth the emotion of love. If we desire them to love a friend or a relative, we tell them of the many noble qualities this friend possesses, and his generous self-sacrificing deeds. We describe his very look, manner, style, voice, and gesture; and as they listen, we see by the kindling eye, the changing countenance, that their hearts beat in unison with ours.

Thus with our Bible histories, read to and with our children. Of ourselves we cannot win them; but as we read the wonderful story of Christ, of his early youth, his generous deeds, and spotless character, his yearning compassion, not willing that any should perish, his love for little children, bidding them come to him, we see the movings of his Spirit in their heart, their affections sweetly going out after God.

By becoming thus familiar with the Bible, the historical and prophetical, as well as the biographical parts of it, they will erect a standard that will be of essential service in the selection of other books and authors—a standard of beauty, purity, and truthfulness, to which their general taste will conform.

Physicians tell us that a variety of food is indispensable to the health of the body. God has given us a generous supply, and we are called upon to choose certain dishes that suit our taste, and others which particularly agree with the system and constitution; the stomach readily digesting them, turning them to blood and bones and flesh, renovating and strengthening the entire body. Thus the mind requires a variety; we should choose such works as are in themselves helpful, suggestive, having a tendency to lead upward; with truth to rest upon, argument sufficient to tax the reasoning powers and enlist the judgment, beauty to awaken the imagination and the fancy, with an easy onward movement, leading thought outward, upward, after something holier, happier, more abiding than can be found in ourselves.

Through the agency of books, we become acquainted with the history of nations and people centuries before us; the rise and fall of empires, the glory of kingdoms, the downfall of states. Individualizing we become interested. We enter into the spirit of the age, understanding the motives and influences brought to bear upon the minds of the leading actors in the great drama of life, winning experience through their mistakes: the whole having a tendency to render us more just, more generous, more charitable. Our range of thought should be broad, vast, comprehensive, and we should think of ourselves as nothing, and still hold ourselves as ennobled by reason of our relation to the Creator; for we are "bought with a price," and should be careful in word, thought, and deed, not to dishonor him.

The study of geology, astronomy, botany, and other natural sciences will disclose to us beauty more wondrous and fascinating than the pen of the novelist ever drew, the glory and majesty of God's works, his treasured storehouse being revealed to us, the secrets of the great deep made known. To engage the minds of our children to follow after things beautiful and good, we must impress them with an earnest persistent desire after what is beautiful and good in our own lives. We must know the way and walk in it, before we can point it out to others.

The choice of authors we must make a personal matter, selecting according to the character, inclination, pursuits, and temper of the child. As no two children are exactly alike in look, temperament, and habit, so each must have of necessity a different way of looking at things, different methods of thought and study. We are not to destroy these individual characteristics, but to train them, turning natural inclination into profitable channels; bringing out ability and passive talent, laying open the understanding to the light of truth, mellowing the sensibilities, and making ready for an abundant harvest.

While it is well to have a book always on hand, fleshless lips ready with a thought or a suggestion, it is absolutely necessary to cultivate a methodical arrangement, a regular course of reading, if we would build up and improve the mind to the highest limit. Neither will it be sufficient to read; we must aid our children to form right habits of thought, judging accurately with respect to the characters they meet with in reading, sifting and analyzing men's aims in life, appropriating what is good, and leaving the chaff, if chaff there be, to the winds of forgetfulness.

These are preliminary preparations, weak and imperfect in themselves, and still helps in the formation of character lasting as eternity.

Another consideration, and one which through the multiplicity of care we too frequently forget, is a specific arrangement with reference to time, a sensible division of duties; with no conflict, no clashing, nothing hurried, nothing omitted. We should cherish order without rudeness, a certain gliding movement showing executive power and ability in guiding the small craft safely.

A habit of reading is one of the best safeguards for our children against temptation; rendering home peculiarly dear to them. As they gather around the study table, the out-door life is for the time forgotten; while the child revels in the sublimity of thought, the beauty of conception, the elevating imagery of the printed pages: perchance travelling through space, calling the stars by name, measuring their distances, noting their changes, studying their nature, conjecturing of their inhabitants; thus the mind is enlarged, and the heart aided to grasp a more tangible idea of the greatness, the power, the love of the great Author.

In contrast with such delights, vice will look less attractive, and folly lose its charm. Time will seem more precious, life more dignified and noble, and the responsible duties of life worthy of more careful consideration.

Sitting by the dancing flittering firelight, Newton reasoned. and Fulton studied, with many others, a long gallery of names of whom the world is justly proud. Not merely the circumstances in life, but a thousand varied influences go to form the child's life, to mould the character: the unconscious influence, the caress, the half-spoken word, the unvoiced rebuke, the speaking, pleading eye, the silent prayer.

In the division of duties we are not to forget a specified season of prayer, an hour set aside to intercede for ourselves and our loved ones at the throne of grace; specifying their names one by one, breathing our hopes, fears, desires into the ear of our heavenly Father; beseeching him by his great mercy to have them in his most holy keeping. Let the children know this hour; let them see how much we lean upon the arm of his love for wisdom to guide and direct us in all that we do. Let them feel how much we value these precious seasons of communion with Christ, in joy or in sorrow going to him freely, talking with him just as they are accustomed to see us talk with our long cherished friends.

A mother who has the happiness of seeing all her sons occupying places of trust and responsibility—all of them, with one exception, converted in early life—made it a practice to kneel with her boys separately: specifying the little daily acts of each one, imploring that the good in his character might be strengthened, the ill blotted out; thus making the Saviour her confidant, and leading her children to feel that whatever was done would be repeated by the mother. On one occasion she was obliged to administer correction to the youngest, leaving him in his room while she went about her ordinary duties. Presently the door opened and a little pleading voice cried:

"Mamma, I'm fretted; let us go and tell Jesus." And not until she led him to the accustomed room, and kneeling with him, told the Saviour just what he had done, could the child feel that the wrong was forgiven.

Such hours with our children are to be looked upon as seasons of communion with God, in which our souls gain new vigor, and from which we are to return filled with that fulness of delight which every soul must feel after an interview with its Beloved.

VI.

What Shall We Sing?

THE question implies that we do sing. Music belongs to the family as much as song to birds, sunshine to flowers, dew to the parched fields. Who ever forgets the music of a mother's voice in a mother's song? or is not, later in life, conscious at times of a secret longing down deep in the heart to be folded once more in the same loving arms, to be rocked to sleep with the same soft lullaby? Why is it that our hearts thrill with rapture as we listen to the grand onward flow of Old Hundred, or Coronation, in the sweet "still hour of prayer," save that a mother's face is hidden there, a mother's voice lingering in the inmost recesses of our hearts? Since we are to have music in heaven, it is well to commence on earth. What so natural to the renewed heart as praise? Joy and gladness bubble up in the heart of a child. Some one has appropriately said: "The Christian life is only a glorified childhood."

If we would have home bright, beautiful, and happy, we must not be afraid to sing. "Make a joyful noise unto God, all ye lands, sing forth the honor of his name: make his praise glorious; all the earth shall worship thee, they shall sing to thy name."

With what feelings of awe and reverence we walk on the shores of the great sea, and listen to the choral chant sweeping up from innumerable waves; the grand "all hail" echoing along the vaulted arch; "the stars singing together," and the sons of God striking their golden harps in unison. The winds like the tread of mighty armies, swelling across the plain, and through the treetops, deep, full, sonorous; then low, sad, plaintive. The song of the breeze and the rain-drops; the flower bells and the lily cups joining in the chorus: "All the earth shall worship thee, they shall sing to thy name."

What recollection is more pleasing than the gatherings at nightfall; the memory of mingled voices blending still closer the harmonies of affection, by the refining influences of this heaven-born art. No one influence will add more to the comfort of home than the cultivation of pure and elevating music. With it children are more easily governed, and its practice is favorable to refinement of thought and elevation of character.

As our little ones grew older we paid more attention to music; their father had a good voice, and I had been said to know something of it in my young days; and with Margaret and Jem to carry a part, we frequently sat in the twilight and sang, not minding if the passers stopped at the gate. Gertrude had a sweet voice, and in her new home she was favored with a rare teacher. Professor Islam was a thorough musician. His soul was full of music bubbling up and running over his lips; every nerve thrilled with melody; his movement was the poetry of song, and loving his art, he loved the Giver; and loving God he loved every created being, and longed with all the fervor of his great generous heart to teach them to sing.

Professor Islam passed by one evening just as we had gathered around the instrument with our evening songs. The voices of the children filled him with a desire to enter. The hour passed on the wings of melody. Hitherto we had been obliged to dispense with a tenor. Although so young, Margaret was a lover of music, and putting her lips to my ear, she begged me to invite the professor to come again. The next day my neighbor called in person. "Would I be so good as to permit Margaret to take lessons of Gertrude's teacher?" It was the very thing I had desired, and renewed cause had we to sing; for His goodness had been round about us—His banner over us had been love.

The family is the nursery of the church. Hence a Christian family must sing with the same spirit in which they pray. Singing is only talking in a different key: "singing with the spirit, and with the understanding." Two spirits cannot prevail in us at the same time, a spirit of praise and thanksgiving, and a spirit of gloom and despondency are not expected to harmonize.

In the selection of music the same conscientious care is required as in reading. If we would shun low, vain, trifling reading, we must not sing low, vain, foolish songs. It is impossible for the soul to rise on the wings of melody if the words are light and frivolous. The charm is not alone in the air, the sentiment must be refined and elevating, or the influence of the melody is lost. In conversation a musical voice heightens the effect, it gives pleasure, we love to listen; but it is the theme that has the power, lifting us above the trivial employments of time, filling the soul with glimpses of what is beyond, strengthening and invigorating by its genial influences and causing the pathway of life to brighten with added loveliness.

As in conversation pictures of nobleness and truth are stamped upon the soul, so with music the words should be pure, elevating, the air inspiring. "Is any merry? let him sing." Is any sad, song has a healing balm. Heaven is described as a place where each inhabitant has a crown and a harp.

Besides the pleasure received, music is an educator; the study of it as a science has as much to do in disciplining the mind as a course in mathematics, or the study of languages. The laws of rhyme, harmony, and counterpoint are not mastered without long and attentive study, laying the foundation for close consecutive thought and well-digested argument.

As a people we have been behind in the study of music; but that day is past. Music is no longer a graft, we may safely consider it an inborn principle, or rather to be drunk in by our children with the air they breathe. Much of this we doubtless owe to the loved authors of Hebron, Uxbridge, and other like modern compositions. All praise to the energy and skill brought to bear upon the turning-point in our musical history. It is to their far-sightedness that we are indebted for the introduction of music into our public schools: while it is still left to us as mothers to introduce it into our families; a tiny golden thread let down from heaven by which our children are to be led along the path of rectitude and honor. Next to prayer, music is the best safeguard; evil thoughts and base purposes cannot enchain a soul accustomed to soar into the divine realm of sacred melody.

It was said by the corn-law rhymer, "Let me make the songs for the people, and I care not who makes the laws."

From Jubal to the present time music has been a powerful instrument to inspire. The soldier is led on to victory by it, the devotion of the Christian is heightened by it, social life is enlivened and polished: while it is to the family a divine messenger of love, stimulating to good works, linking heart to heart, and binding with a threefold cord to the throne of God.

The love and practice of music tend to benevolence, just as the love of God in the soul does away with caste and exclusive privilege.

"Mamma," said Margaret as she came from her lesson, her face aglow with enthusiasm, "Professor Islam says it can be done."

"What can be done, my child?"

"The little musical entertainment that you and papa were speaking of."

"You asked him?"

'Was it wrong, mamma?" and the blue eyes grew misty, "I did so want the money, and if we sing for it, it will be ours to give; and mamma," coming very near and leaning her head on my shoulder, "God will think more of it, gained in this way, than he would if papa was rich and could give it to us."

We had been talking of a mission-school in connection with our regular church work, but funds were wanting, and looking about for ways and means a musical entertainment or concert by our little band was suggested. It only needed my neighbor's influence and the professor's leadership to insure success, and this the children had obtained.

In all plans of benevolence we were in the habit of allowing the children to share. Thus their interest was enlisted, and the habit of giving, or of dividing what they had with those who had less, was established. Not alone for the mission-school but daily as we met, Margaret and Gertrude joined in singing the standard hymns and tunes, the little waifs chiming in with great spirit and abandon.

In every heart there is a germ of love for the good and the beautiful, and it is to cultivate this germ, to awaken the desire in the soul for something higher, holier, more abiding, that we are to work. As Christians, in whatever department or of whatever age, we need to praise more; joy sitting in our hearts, the language of thankfulness on our lips, bursting into song in view of His great kindness, His long suffering, the tenderness of His great love.

To sing with the heart and with the understanding is at all times attractive, interesting, and profitable.

VII.

The Friends That We Make.

LOOKING into the mirror of God's word, we find specific rules with reference to the friends that we make, the intimacies that tighten around us, the influences that mould and fashion. Especially is this to be considered in youth, at the time when habits are formed and the foundations of character laid. As mothers we have seen how easily the good resolve was weakened through associations with a genial but unprincipled companion. An evening passed in questionable society has been the ruin of many a youth.

"Can a man take fire in his bosom and his clothes not be burned? Can one go on hot coals and his feet not be burned?" showing plainly the effect of intimate relationship between the vicious and the good: "for what fellowship hath righteousness with unrighteousness? and what communion hath light with darkness? and what concord hath Christ with Belial? or what part hath he that believeth with an infidel?" "And what agreement hath the temple of God with idols? for ye are the temple of the living God." "Wherefore come out from among them, and be ye separate, saith the Lord." "And ye shall be my sons and daughters, saith the Lord Almighty."

The line of demarcation between the godly and the ungodly is a distinct one. It cannot be broken down. In the world, but not of it, the followers of One who went about doing good, the friend of publicans and sinners, we are to imitate Him, "doing good as we have opportunity;" not holding ourselves utterly aloof from the erring, but careful in our associations that we are the leaders, not the led; not in any wise overcome of evil.

There is a love of complacency, and a love of benevolence; the former we give to those whom we term our friends, persons of like habits and feelings, their peculiar qualities of heart and mind reaching a deeper and more intimate part of us, adapting themselves with a nice fit and adjustment to what is characteristic in us, so that they are bound to us and we to them by strong and sacred ties.

The love of benevolence implies that we love, with a readiness to do good, every creature that God has made. If evil, so much the more do we strive to do them good; lost sheep of the same flock, whom we are with all kindness to find and to lead back to the Shepherd from whom they have strayed. As in our dwellings we have different guest chambers, so with the heart chambers it is the privilege of but few to enter the inner sanctuary. Loving all, and ready to lay down his life for the most unworthy, Jesus had a few friends whom he loved with a still tenderer feeling. John is spoken of as "the beloved;" while a peculiar friendship Jesus manifested for that small family in Bethany.

If we would arm our children with full and complete knowledge, we must not shield them from contact with the outer world: temptation is a test of virtue. Standing on the bank the boy will never learn to swim. If he would know his strength, he must dive into the deep water, he must accustom himself to the effort, and it will not be long ere he looks upon the waves with a fearless eye: he has learned how to breast them.

The black waves of sin are seething all around us. If we would have part in the great ingathering, we must begin, we must suffer our children to begin. Much good has been accomplished through the ministry of the little ones. There is little danger but the Father will protect us and ours when we are occupied with his business. God does not promise exemption from suffering, neither from temptation. His promise is to be with us, his grace sufficient in times of sorest need.

As mothers, we cannot expect to remain long with our children. In his providence we may soon be called to leave them. At best, just as they are fitted to be our companions, our helpers, we are expected to give them, one by one, to the guardianship of others, going out from us to build up homes for themselves. A dear-bought privilege, "to bear, to rear, and to lose." Little clinging arms! never is the mother's heart so full of sacred joy, as when she feels your clasping, looks down into the dancing eyes, the rosy dimpled mouth reposing so trustingly on her breast. Messengers of love lent, not given, to be trained and polished for "cornerstones." Loving, is it not a mistake to pamper them too much? to hedge them round with so much luxury that the loss of it would leave them oarless and helmless, or stranded and broken by the tide?

If we would see our daughters polished and beautiful, we must train them for the battle of life. God's jewels are refined in the furnace, they are cut with the keen blade of sorrow, they are filed and polished by a long weary process, and only by this are they fitted for the crown.

The family is God's workshop; precious jewels are here to go through the polishing process, and a portion of the work is assigned to us. Instead of keeping them in the tower like the crown jewels of England, we are to teach them, that although young, they are not too young to exert a good influence over those with whom they have to do; to show them the difference between the sweet personal intercourse of kindred minds, and the large-hearted open benevolence felt for all, especially the aged, the infirm, the helplessly poor and neglected.

The want of reverence is a crying sin of our times. As mothers, cannot we teach our children that respect is due the hoary head? Cannot we teach them that to listen is in itself an accomplishment unrivalled by its opposite "to talk well"? Cannot we show them that the sweetest lessons of piety and wisdom are to be drawn from sources having but little in the exterior to claim the eye?

When Jesus was upon earth he was the friend of the poor and the needy, the low, even the wicked, lost, doomed malefactor. He did not shut himself up in a palace, he had not even a cottage home, he lacked needed comfort; he was cold and hungry, but never diverted from his great work; he saw the way, he knew the agony that was before him. But no, he could not turn back. The cup given him he must drink, bitter though it be: great drops of agony standing on that pure brow, like drops of blood.

All this was for us, it was for our children. In settling the question with regard to the friends that we make, let us aim first of all to make a friend of Jesus; not a nominal friend, but a companion, known, loved, honored, and confided in. Let us not rest satisfied until each of our children has won the lasting friendship of this same Jesus. Trusting in him, and guided by his precepts, we cannot go astray in making to ourselves earthly friends. If we love him we shall not be inclined to take into the inner sanctuary of the heart one who does not regard Him whom our soul loveth. What communion could there be? linked but still apart; drinking at different cisterns: eating, but not of the same bread.

If we would be eager to secure the friendship of Jesus for our children, let us in their very babyhood give them in prayer and faith to him; claiming the promise, "all things whatsoever ye shall ask in prayer believing, ye shall receive;" teaching them in all things, so that their walk may be in keeping with the written word.

A mother who had brought up a large family of children, all of whom had become members of the Christian fold, was asked what means she had used with so much success, to win them to the cross. She replied: "I have always felt that if they were not converted before they became seven or eight years of age, they would probably be lost; and when they have approached that age, I have been in an agony lest they should pass it unconverted. I have gone to the Lord in my anguish, and he has not turned away my prayers, nor his mercy from me."

Oh, the happiness of such a mother! The sweet communion of such a family, heaven begun upon earth—living and working to promote the same object, seeking the poor, the weak, the miserable, and leading them to Jesus. To the old and hardened in sin, little children are angel ministers; their sweet lispings of Jesus touch the obstinate heart. They listen as they would not to the mature Christian; they confide in the trusting child-love; they do not think of questioning, they do not suspect artifice; and often, the arrow once lodged in their hearts, they do not rest till they have found an interest in the same Saviour.

God does not need man's intellect; the power of his Spirit is not shown through the wisdom of this world. "Out of the mouth of babes and sucklings hast thou ordained strength." The smallest stars are nearest to the great centre, little arms cling the closest, and little children often excel us; their simple artless questions are like nails fastened in a sure place. In Gertrude's home, her frequent entertainments are given. Had I been skeptical with reference to what a child can do, I should have been convinced by seeing what she has already accomplished.

Colonel H—— had just returned from a long residence abroad. A man of rare native ability and inheriting large wealth, he was favored with extensive mental culture. Universities and colleges bestowed their favors, and society offered a charmed cup. Elegant in manner, fascinating in appearance, Colonel H—— was an infidel. His understanding could not take in the sublime truths of the gospel, and because he could not comprehend, he scouted it entirely, and for years the Bible was to him a sealed book. Colonel H—— made his home in the family by whom Gertrude was adopted. His heart was won by the sweet beauty of the child, and when she slid her hand into his and asked him to go with her to church, and to the mission-school, he could not refuse. The idea of good was not in his heart. A man of the world, petted by society, with a balanced mind and well-established principles, to be led by a child! No, of course he would never change; but Gertrude asked him, and he loved the child.

Months passed. Colonel H—— was ill, nigh unto death. His little friend was with him, her sensitive nature was touched, and in her sweet artless manner did she ask Jesus in behalf of her sick friend. As he grew better she curled herself up beside him, and read from her small Bible. She told him of Jesus, her own precious friend. Her manner was simple and direct; the heart of the invalid was tender, he saw the preciousness of such a Friend, he longed to claim him for his own.

"Only love him," whispered Gertrude.

"But will he let me?"

"I love you!" whispered Gertrude.

"But Jesus I have slighted for so many years, I am afraid that he will refuse me now!"

"Afraid of Jesus! Why it's because you do n't know him. All the days that you was ill, he was right here; I used to ask him for you every day, and he loved you, or he would n't have let you get well. Do love him just a little bit;" and burying her face in the pillow the little one wept.

It was a new idea to Colonel H——. Did he in reality owe his life to Jesus? and the question once started could not be put aside. A breach once made, the strong barrier of infidelity gradually crumbled away, the strong man saw himself a sinner in the sight of God, an ingrate, lost, ruined, undone, without a Mediator. For a time he was almost in despair. "I, even I, am he that comforteth you," whispered Gertrude. "Though your sins be as scarlet, they shall be white as snow; though they be red like crimson, they shall be as wool." Blessed little teacher, leading the man of intellect to Jesus. Well might Colonel H—— say, as he did say in giving in his Christian experience, "It was not by might, neither the wisdom of the world, nor the pride of intellect; but by his Spirit and the teaching of a little child."

VIII.

Self-Denial.

THE lesson of self-denial is of the utmost importance in laying the groundwork of a good, noble character for our children. Self, and the importance that attaches to personal gratification, is a weed of such strong growth, that unless early attention is given it, a judicious pruning and lopping of the overgrown leaves, they will effectually shut out the sunshine from the flowers, and mar their beauty and harmony.

Surely, some one says, we are not to expect our children to understand the true principles of self-denial, and understanding, thus be brought to practise it. Why not? Is not the germ of goodness the same? The oak was once a sapling; the man was once a babe: in either case the change was gradual. The sapling grew and was counted by years; the babe grew slowly, by degrees. When the oak was a sapling, it could be swayed and bent and made to grow straight or crooked. By a process known to gardeners, it could have been dwarfed, and still have been harmonious in all its parts. Unnatural as such a growth would be, it would have remained an oak. No process could change its nature.

Is it not thus with the child? Like the sapling, can he not be swayed and bent and made to grow straight or crooked? In either case, if we would have a perfect development, there must be no forced growth. To train is all that is required. As in the oak all the limbs do not make their appearance at the same time, so in the child the inclinations and native tendencies do not show themselves at once. Selfishness is radical, however; the babe in our arms gives ample proof. Look how he clutches the toy; he will not yield it. "Mine, mine!" he cries, and hugging it in his arms, he exerts his strength to retain it. True, some children show more of this propensity than others; but on every page of human nature self is written in characters more or less defined. This principle is needful to an extent. We do not wish to destroy and uproot it, but to prune and tend it, keeping it under; for if left to run wild, it will so shadow the virtues as materially to affect the fruit.

Looking into the sacred volume, we find that self-denial is made the condition of discipleship by our Saviour, so that, unless in some degree we practise it, our claim to the character and privileges of Christians is invalid. But what is its nature?

Self-denial, when practised through love or for the sake of a loved object, has nothing austere or ascetic. It does not call for pilgrimages, hardships, and seclusion; neither has it a sour look and crabbed appearance. By self-denial, we mean a persevering effort to conform desire, appetite, and temper to the requirement of God's word; content with our lot, resigned to providential appointment, submissive to God as to a Father.

But why must our children deny themselves? So that they may early acquire this grace, esteeming others better than themselves, giving with a generous hand, finding pleasure in seeing others happy. Otherwise they may grow up to be penurious, grasping, forgetful that the Father of mercies not only beholds, but graciously promises to reward the good that is done in his name; teaching our children not only to embrace opportunities to do good, but to create them, and be thus always abounding in the work of the Lord.

The boy that divides his books or his toys with those who have less, not only does a praiseworthy act, but he is laying the foundation for a noble, generous manhood. The girl that gives her doll to the sick child of a poor neighbor, reaps a pleasure that she could not from any other source, and will most likely grow into a full, free, generous-hearted woman.

Many parents are in the habit of giving freely, and also lead their children to give in the same munificent manner. Said a lady, "I never knew any thing of the spirit of self-denial until I was under the necessity of earning for myself. As a child, I was in the habit of giving freely; but it was of my superfluity. Did I give any thing to the cause of humanity, my parents took occasion to supply me with something more valuable, and more highly prized because of its freshness."

We need not say that there is nothing of self-denial in such giving. Whatever the circumstances of the parent, in order to learn the lesson of self-denial the gift of the child must be coupled with personal effort or sacrifice. Above all, he is to feel that it is for Christ's sake. If he has already given himself to Christ, it will not require many words to convince him of the beauty as well as of the necessity of doing good without selfishness.

God loves a cheerful giver. Let the object of our bounty see that it is love that inspires us. The kindness with which a favor is bestowed will double the value of it with a grateful receiver.

Hence the beautiful exhortation, "He that giveth, let him do it with simplicity;" that is, without extolling or debasing his gift; without ostentation, without pride. Let our children understand that God expects us to give according to our means; pennies will not do for one who has pounds. The gift of a flower, a leaf, if one has nothing more, has power to mould character and to form habit.

Merely giving is but a small part of what is understood by self-denial. In every family, not a day but calls for the practice of this virtue—at the table and in the parlor, the small preferences, the cosiest chair at the fire, the favorite seat at the window, the coveted place on papa's knee, the seat in the carriage when all cannot go, the rare fruit or delicate viand. On occasions like these, how beautiful to observe the spirit of self-denial, the oldest giving preference to the youngest, the strongest to the weakest, each vying with the other for the pleasure and practice of self-denial.

If our children are thus accustomed in their youth, may we not expect that they will not depart from such a course, as they grow to be men and women, in their turn to teach and to lead others?

In almost every neighborhood there are families more or less destitute, people of genuine worth in many respects, but crippled for the want of means; without friends, without books, without every thing save the bare necessaries of life. An occasional call, a few books left as a loan, a garment fitted and made to look becomingly, a few words of friendly advice or suggestion, cost nothing save a little self-denial, and throw a world of sunshine over the humble home.

In every locality, and especially among the destitute, there are more or less children unable to go to school. Could there be a purer pleasure than to gather these little waifs into a comfortable room and instruct them, teaching them to sew, to knit, as well as to read and study? A little self-denial by one who has the leisure, and the entire neighborhood is remodelled and made to wear a very different aspect.

Many a sick-room has been brightened, the heart of the sufferer filled with hope, the hands strengthened, by the timely aid that came through the practice of self-denial by a prosperous neighbor. Little deeds like these done by our children, will be worth to them more than houses and lands without them. Life is not long enough to indulge in selfishness; and still, to do good is not a natural growth; it is the effect of teaching. This spirit fostered in our homes tends to broad and enlightened views.

Visiting the sick and the suffering, a habit of listening is formed—no mean accomplishment, as may be found in after years; and also the power of winning attention—an easy assimilation and adaptation to others and to their groove of thought. The mind needs unresisting, merely listening attention for its development; and this is found on reading to those whose understanding, for the want of culture, does not enable them to detect flaws or to make criticisms, but merely to enjoy, and in a measure to profit by what is given them.

It is an aphorism worthy of a deep and permanent impression on our hearts, that self-denial is the source of our highest gratification.

IX.

School Life.

THERE is no more critical period in childhood, perhaps, than when the question of school and school duties is first agitated; when we send our children away from our immediate care and protection, and share the labor and responsibility with another, and that other a stranger, but partially known at best, and frequently not at all.

It had been our care to instruct the children. Margaret could read and write correctly, and Jem was ready for Latin; Maude had outgrown the name of "baby;" a last year's nursling was in my arms; and with such increase of care, I could no longer do justice to their lessons. The question had frequently been asked, and now we felt it must be answered, "Can we place our children among strangers? Shall we keep them at home, or send them to the public school?" Each plan had its advantages and its drawbacks. Margaret and Jem were not widely divided in their studies; they had been in the same class. We did not like to separate them. We could not think of sending them from home. Each would serve as mentor to the other—Jem's mirth toned down to a gentle decorum by his sister's speech; while Maude would lean upon both, and at home I should feel better satisfied.

Try as I would, it was hard to see them go; and holding Birdie up, my hungry eyes followed them out of sight—"away from all who love them." It was their first step into the world, and a quick pang shot through my heart as they went—Margaret with her tender eyes, and Jem noble and manly, as he always had been at home; but I knew him to be quick and irascible, feeling intensely, and sometimes rash, but when he did a wrong so truly sorry; and stretching out my arms, I longed to take him—to take them all to my sheltering heart.

It was a quick thought, and shot upward like a flame, wrapping me in with doubts and fears, and almost murmurings. How could I let them go, my priceless jewels? What if stain or long and ugly scar should mar the work? The tears streamed down my face. The work was mine to rear and train them all; to fit them for the world, and thus for a place in heaven. I could not hope to keep them with me. At best the path through life would be a tangled one. But He in whom we trusted would lead and guide and teach. It was a sweet thought, and all at once my mind was calm. My babes were His to keep, and mine to teach them not to wander from his side.

As the sun went down the children came from school, a certain awe and wonder in their eyes; so much they had to tell, and Maude was very sure she 'd love the little girl "in the red dress and pretty soft brown hair;" and the teacher was kind and good, like mamma. I took her to my heart and hugged her close, my blue-eyed Maude; and a yearning love went out to that fair teacher, "kind and good, like mamma."

Jem told us of the sports at recess, and that he could run as fast as the fastest, and throw a ball; and cricket he could learn, did papa think it suitable for such a boy. All the time Margaret's face wore a look of such sweet gravity. I could not but kiss the child, and ask of the lessons, Were they difficult and hard to learn? With this she opened her Latin grammar, pointing to "Amo." "That is all, and Jem must take 'Musa.'" It was a pleasant evening running through "Amo;" first papa and myself, then Margaret, and at last Jem's facile tongue rang out the changes on "Musa" as though it had been his mother tongue.

The next day I was happier, sending my thought out on a pleasanter track. Gertrude was with them, and Professor Islam was to give vocal lessons in the same school. And their influence, if we were careful to keep it pure at home, would show itself like some clear stream; at first a tiny brook, but widening as it grew, freshening the fields and giving beauty to the wayside flowers. Was not this our end and aim? And thus far God had blessed us. Why distrust? I grew to loathe my fear, and pressed near to ask for gifts. I held his promise, "Ask," and I knew his word could never fail.

As school life advanced, we became more intimately acquainted with the teachers, and my heart went out to this class as it had never done before. I saw that some held teaching as a high and sacred office, and others looked upon it as a means to live. But why expect any class, or all of a class, to be free from fault? A teacher's responsibility is only second to that of the mother; and as mothers we see much in our own hearts that we would have otherwise. Motives are the criterion, however, and that one does most good who uniformly acts from the highest, purest motives.

It was said by a man of eminent worth that every step of life is a discipline, every breath a refiner. Pleasant as student life may be, it has its dangers. Ambitious to excel, the scholar not unfrequently runs into gross error; and to hide this he practises still another, and another, until he becomes an adept in duplicity and falsehood in every degree, and for every purpose. It is so easy, if the pupil has a difficult or a disagreeable duty, to stay away from class; and if the reason is asked, as it is sure to be, to plead illness is almost natural when the pupil understands that an engagement will not answer. If the rules are so stringent as only to be satisfied with a written communication from the parent, it is easy to ask and obtain an excuse. Otherwise the daughter herself writes, signs her mother's name, and it is done. The first instance, conscience most likely cries out against it as unjust, dishonorable, and highly injurious to the pupil.

The next, the voice is less strong, and at length it ceases to speak.

To excel in composition is a natural desire; fancy is excited, imagination stimulated, intellect awakened. The effusion of the youthful writer is praised; prophets rise up, and down the future the young aspirant for literary honors sends her gaze; lights are flashing, and garlands of beauty to crown her brow. With extended research, she clips to suit herself, and before she is aware she has dropped from the height she was so sure to win.

Perhaps there is no time when we should so closely attach ourselves to our daughters as during the period of school life, offering ourselves as companions, studying with them, sympathizing with them, winning their confidence. Naturally demonstrative, the school girl must have some one to love and to confide in.

With a character still unformed, she cannot herself judge of her associates except so far as the exterior is concerned. A sad thing if she has not a mother who can be touched with her need, who can enter into all her petty trials, who can understand the peculiar temptations liable to meet her every day; a mother willing to watch the springs of action, keeping the soul from the miasma of wrong influence by well-timed speech and example.

Many a young girl has taken her first downward step while at school. Susceptible and easily pleased, she often forms acquaintances that are worse than profitless. At first it is only a chance meeting going to and from school; then growing bolder, her new friend lends her books, or offers a bouquet. Nothing could be more respectful. The girl is unsuspecting; but the chain is being forged that will tighten around the delicate form, and at last sink her with its terrible weight.

As mothers, we have need of all our powers. While we sit idle the enemy is sowing tares. The great Gardener who gave us this vine to train will come to question us with reference to our work. The gem given us to polish will be required at our hands. The bird we were to teach to sing will be wanting in paradise, if we are unfaithful.

These are but few of the avenues whereby wrong creeps into student life. Not unfrequently the love of dress is fostered; vanity fed into a flame; romance and sentiment give false views of the reality and responsibility of life. Said a pious woman, in speaking of her daughter: "I consider the period of school-girl life the most beautiful and the most dangerous in the path of woman." If this is true, and our own experience goes to sustain it, must we not seek to lay the foundation before our daughters go from us?

Perhaps there is no one thing that needs more careful watch than the so-called recreation, the unbending from study, the refreshment and diversion, the picking up a book light as foam and brilliant with false glare. Such reading, although but momentary, tends to deaden the soul, to dwarf the intellect, to benumb the senses, leaving the imagination to take the lead; and thus the advantages of which the student might have availed herself prove only swift messengers leading down to death. Said a mother, in speaking of the popular romances of the day: "I am thankful that my daughter does not read them."

"Are you sure?" asked a friend, who understood the child much better than the mother did.

"Oh, yes, I am sure; she gives her time to her lessons. I have been particularly careful. She never reads novels."

Deception was perfect in this case; the mother did not know. A conscientious woman, she did not dream that her daughter would read by stealth, devoting study hours to her lessons, and sitting up half the night poring over books sure to leave stains on her soul.

Another evil, but happily not so frequent as years ago, is an undue love of study. Led on by conscientious motives, anxious to make the most of present opportunity, the poor girl studies, heedless of law, unknowing, at least unthinking, that if nature is taxed wrongfully, she will be avenged. Neither will the mind bear consecutive hours of unbroken study. Progress is not of forced growth. So much as the mind can digest, patiently persevered in, will accomplish the desire;

but study that becomes a tax, through weariness of brain and muscle, does no good; more than this, it clogs the brain, and therefore weakens it. As a rule, in mental effort, when weary, rest is necessary. To sit passive is not always required; change gives the mind a respite. In this way thought will strengthen, the taxed energies regain their vigor; and the advance will be all the more marked for what at first may seem lost time.

True, there are cases where the strength and activity of the mental powers hold the body in abeyance—souls that sit and sing, regardless of the frail tenement that shelters them; but these are exceptions. God may have a work for such, and will care for them. Cannot we teach our daughters the happy mean, and at length have the satisfaction of seeing them ruddy and strong, yet with minds vigorous, well cultivated, and quick to grasp great and essential truths? Cannot we teach them, that the responsibility of woman's life calls for health of body and a well-disciplined mind; that good sense and strong nerves are preferable to a weak sentimentality, a shattered, irritable nervous system? God has given us a world of beauty, and he has so ordered it that the path, however humble, is not destitute of enjoyment. The way cannot be lonely that is brightened by his presence; the heart that is filled with his love has no cause for uneasiness. To advance in mental culture, and secure a growth of grace in the soul, reaching out after what is holier and higher; not unmindful to teach and to lead; in all things good showing herself a pattern; this is the grand aim and end of woman's life.

X.

Habit.

IF childhood is the time to lay foundations, the forming time for strong pure character and abiding principle, it is likewise the time for habit to fasten itself: a mere trifle, an excrescence that at first can be removed easily; but if permitted to harden it cannot be amputated without the knife and the danger at least of a scar. In our children we see little idiosyncrasies peculiar to this or that parent or relation; a certain peculiarity so exact that it is noticeable, and we exclaim, "How very like!" the look, expression, or fac-simile of the person in question. In other instances it is an imitation, a parasite attaching itself to us, sure to cling and to grow. It may come from Bridget in the kitchen or Patrick at the stable; or it may come from the nursery-maid or her street acquaintance. Where it originated is of secondary importance; it is there. To remove it is our work. It may be the squint of the eye, a peculiar curl to the lip, an unpleasant shrug of the shoulders, a wry face, stammering, one or all of these; like the measles or smallpox, of slight importance if attended to in time; but allowed to increase, dangerous to the well-being of the child.

Habit does not attach itself to the outward exclusively; slang phrases and low forms of speech, especially when flavored with witticism, find quick appreciation with children. The half-formed expression, meaningless as they use it, not unusually provokes merriment, causing a laugh that encourages them to attempt it again. Such a course, if persisted in, may close the child's mind to any thing better. Like his seniors, he loves to be applauded; and if by using a cant expression or a slang phrase he succeeds in winning a laugh, be sure that he will repeat it, and before you are aware, he becomes an adept, his entire speech of the same type and quality.

With the gardener it is not enough that he prunes and lops; not a day escapes but he looks and examines. The more valuable the vine the closer is his scrutiny: change of temperature will affect it; too much sunshine and too little moisture wither it; insects may ruin it, or dust disfigure it. It is the business of the gardener to keep it fresh and vigorous, and he gives it the needful care.

Is it not thus with the plants growing about our doors? general pruning and culture are not sufficient, we must watch closely, lest some rude unsightly thing mar the beauty of the leaf, or eat into the heart of the bud. We cannot leave them to other hands, we cannot rest without knowing for ourselves that they are safe.

Especially do we see the effect of habit when our children begin to associate with others at school or on the street. A new thing it was to see Jem come into the parlor, his hat tipped to one side, his hands in his pockets, an easy do n't-care manner, whistling as he goes.

"Why, Jem, you forget yourself. Mamma would not like to see you come in in this manner," said Margaret.

It does no good; Jem whistles only the louder.

"Howard Paul never takes off his hat

in the house, and he whistles. He says it's being cheerful."

It's being cheerfuller not to do it, I should think," and Maude chimes in, running up to Jem and attempting to lift his hat.

"No, you don't;" and Jem straightens himself up, and throws back his head.

Jem had no idea that mamma saw this new exhibition of manliness; but he tried to look brave.

"Did my little boy ever see papa enter the parlor with his hands in his pockets, whistling, and wearing his hat?"

"I never do so away from home; it don't matter with only us."

"So it don't matter if you make mamma and the little sisters unhappy."

"Such little things shouldn't make anybody unhappy."

"Have you forgotten what papa was

telling us about the temple, how every little block fitted into its place, with no two blocks just alike. Have you forgotten?"

"No, mamma;" and Jem's eyes were full of tears; "I know what you would say, our bodies are temples, and every thing we do makes them beautiful or it makes them ugly, and this makes me ugly;" and flinging his arms around my neck, he hid his brown face in my dress.

An impulsive child, I tremble for him; and still he is quick to feel, and sorry for a fault. Howard Paul is a dearly loved playmate, petted by a too-indulgent aunt that stands to him in the relation of mother. I sometimes wish that he lived not so near; but Howard has no mother, and my heart yearns over him. What would become of Jem if petted like Howard Paul?

There is a habit of saying disagreeable things, that sometimes creeps into the family circle; an undue love of teazing, that if fostered will grow into a habit by no means praiseworthy. Not only children, but grown people fall into this habit, always ready to make known an unwelcome truth: people who pride themselves on saying what they think, regardless of another's feelings; their conscience quieted, if indeed it is disturbed, by saying, "Well, it is true." As though the truth could be proclaimed at any time, and in all circumstances.

"Why did you tell Miss Wise that her hair was gray?" "Because it is." "Why remind Mrs. Hartley that her dress was faded?" "I saw it." "Why did you refer to that article in the newspaper when S—— was near?" "Because I had just read it." "Why did you tell Putnam that you met his old chum and rival?" "For the reason that

I did meet him." Candid and true; but why say it? raking up old wounds and canker-sores in the room of sitting in the sunshine of pleasant thoughts and friendly interchange of views and feelings. Many who unconsciously have the habit of saying disagreeable things, are in the main well-meaning people. They have no idea how their words cut; they are disappointed, and, looking for blemishes, they are sure to find them.

True, there are occasions when the truth must be told, independent of personal feeling; for instance, when justice is to be done to an injured or accused party, or when, through ambiguity, there is misunderstanding that can be put right by a few timely words. But this is very different from the habit of saying disagreeable things with a spirit of malice, or even of sport, and for the sake of lessening enjoyment.

The grand centre for the display of this habit is the domestic hearth; where, giving loose rein to disappointed feeling, unawed by strangers and unrestrained by laws of good breeding, parents and children, brothers and sisters, scatter words that burn into the heart and brain, and think no more of it than of eating their daily food. Unpleasant as this picture is, it is not overdrawn. We all have known families where the individual members, if not absolutely rude and disagreeable in their daily intercourse, were far from being as pleasant and as kind as to strangers. If this is the habit of the parent, we can scarcely blame the children if they fall into the same habit.

In teaching our children that home is the place to exhibit good breeding, we must not fail to show them that genuine politeness belongs rather to the heart than to the head. The true code of etiquette is found in the Bible; the rules are brief and easily remembered. The spirit of politeness is essentially the spirit of the gospel, gentle, kind, tender, charitable, "in honor preferring one another." By teaching our children this code, and being careful ourselves to abide by it, habits will be formed which will render home happier, and give a new charm to social influence. In order to establish this spirit we must have the confidence of our children, meeting them as friends to whom they can whisper their inmost thoughts. As companions adapting ourselves to their preferences and sympathies, winning them to rely upon our judgment, to trust in our taste, to be satisfied with our arrangements. This intimate companionship is the only way that we can know our children thoroughly, reading their thoughts in the expression of their countenances, and wisely adapting our words to the necessities of each.

Love is not only a polisher, but it is the lamp that brings to light rare powers of mind and soul. Genius is a plant of delicate growth; and talent needs the sweet appreciation of love to stimulate exertion. We may not know the full value of the encouragement we give our children. A trifling assistance in a hard lesson; the easy rendering of a translation; disentangling a problem in geometry; explaining, in a simple manner, a philosophic argument or a chemical experiment: these are little things in themselves, but mighty in their influences.

To do this effectively our minds must be stored with knowledge. It will not answer to say that we have studied. Study must be habitual. We must not suffer ourselves to fall behind the spirit of the age. To keep pace with the young fresh minds around us, we must keep our intellects bright and our hearts active, alive, glowing. Care, anxiety, fretfulness, repining, must not be suffered to spoil the sweet influences of home. Leading others, we must ourselves be led, looking to God continually—each thought a supplication, each breath a prayer. We must permit our children to see, that active and resolute as we are in the world, to them we are always kind and considerate, benevolent and charitable; that there is a mystic inner chamber into which they alone can enter, where heaven is brought nearer, with its glorious hopes; so that they shall be stimulated, encouraged, and led up through the inner sanctuary of a mother's heart.

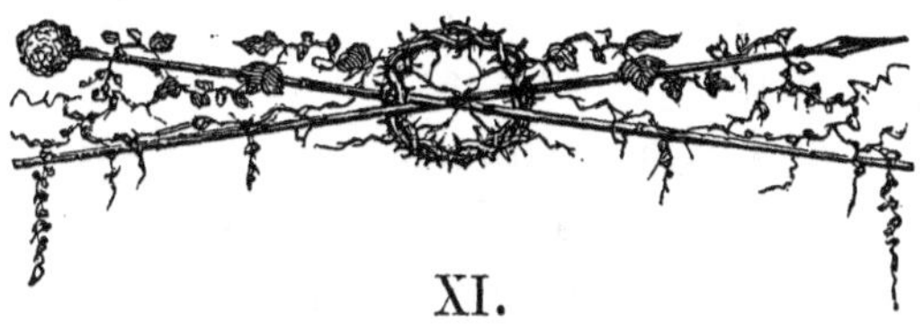

XI.

Conversation.

BY conversation, we do not mean here any thing beyond the easy, familiar intercourse of everyday life. In this the children are to have a part; to be free to speak their thoughts or to ask questions, provided they do it in a respectful, courteous manner, and with due regard to the proprieties of time and place. Children are men and women in miniature; they think, see, and feel very much as their seniors think, see, and feel, with the advantage that the child has of living in a world bright, radiant, joyous. To him every thing is beautiful. A philosopher in his way, he grasps all that he is able to digest, and enjoys without surfeit. Every day his curiosity is fed with a display of mechanism that he cannot understand, marvels of beauty that he cannot unravel. The reflection in the mirror leads the infant to look behind it—a strange wonder on his face as he finds nothing but a plain board with dust and spiders' webs. The murmur of the shell hushes him into quiet, and his eager little mind cannot be satisfied unless he finds the singer. Alas, the shell is ruined, and our little philosopher is no wiser. Violently to repress the feeling of such a child is to injure him for life. Listen patiently to his questions; there is wisdom in them, and the answer will not always be as easy a matter as we sometimes think.

Families there are where the children

creep in and out of the rooms, shy, timid, if a stranger enters; or wild and boisterous, taking the advantage it would seem, when visitors are by, to enjoy a little liberty without fear of rebuke or punishment. If we would have our children civil when guests are in the house, we must teach them to be amiable in the home circle. If we would have them speak becomingly, we must permit them to speak freely; the stream that is dammed up will, when it breaks away, rush with maddening force across the valley: undue repression has the same effect upon the child; and when he breaks away, as he surely will, a wild, boisterous life may be the result.

Speech is the natural avenue of thought; it is the means by which we become acquainted with our friends, making ourselves familiar with them and their peculiar forms of thought. This is the charm of friendship; a fitting in of two natures by an easy, mutual adaptation to each other, harmonizing and blending them so that though different and individual, they are still by this mystical adaptation wrought into a degree of oneness, like the waves of the great deep.

Ties of relationship are not always the bond for such intimate soul union; indeed, a union of soul exists frequently where there is no such relationship. But is this incompatible with the relation in which we stand to our children? Cannot we gain and keep the sweet, pure confidence of childhood? Cannot we take them into our hearts as friends, adapting ourselves to their wants and needs, sharing with them those choice gifts and warmer intimacies that will call out responsive qualities on their part? Our children are our mirrors, reflecting our own moods and inequalities, as well as the nobler attributes of our nature. If we would stand to them in the place of mother, friend, companion, we must talk with them as well as to them. We must listen with easy, artless, unconscious attention, as their very being is unwound and laid before us. Then and then only are we in possession of a knowledge that will enable us to help them day by day; and in our efforts to profit our children, we shall ourselves be profited.

Not long since we were invited to spend a day with a lady of most estimable general character. Her house was duly ordered, her dinner unexceptionable, her manner sweetly affectionate, her conversation elevating; but her children, two attractive little girls, seemed like strangers. At length, after much coaxing, I succeeded in making a slight acquaintance. But while the little one received my caresses she seldom spoke, and then with a covert, painful look, as though she expected a rebuke if she opened her lips. In the course of the evening conversation turned upon home, and the delight we all feel in seeing children bright and happy.

"Your children are extremely quiet," I ventured to remark.

"Quiet because I keep them quiet; they would be wild as hawks if I let them have their own way."

"Then it is their nature to be bright and gay."

"Always asking questions, never still; I never saw such children; it would just take all my time to answer them."

"If you should take the time, would it not cause their lives to run in a smoother and more even groove? Would not their little minds be relieved, their thoughts run out on pleasant subjects, and their hearts be sensibly brightened?"

"Surely you do not think that I wrong my children by trying to keep them quiet and well-behaved?" said the lady.

"I was thinking that it was possible you did not take sufficient pains to become thoroughly acquainted with their individual nature, making friends of them, and talking with them in the same easy, graceful, elevating manner you talk with me."

"Of course not; children are not expected to understand these things."

"The heart of the child longs for sympathy and love in the little engagements of life, as much as the mother longs for sympathy and love in the duties that devolve upon her. Questions that the mother can readily answer, weigh heavily on the young spirit; and the small but uncared-for needs pressing back upon the brain, will not only dwarf intellectual growth and vigor, but will promote inequalities of temper and character."

"But my children are young; as they grow older I see that they will require more."

"More in quantity; the quality of the mind and heart will be the same. Sympathy is what they need, the grand inspirer and mainspring in our common nature."

"Perhaps I have erred in this matter. I did not think that children felt the need of sympathy the same as those who are older."

"Watch your child as she plays with her dolls. Did you ever see her soil a dress or break an arm? Look at the tears, the anguish in the small, upturned face. She runs to you for sympathy; she will never know more real sorrow, she will never more highly appreciate your love. She will remember it. It will mould and fashion her future life."

Are not too many mothers following the example of this one, feeling that their children are too young to be treated to all the little amenities of social life? Thus their eager questions remain unanswered, the warm tide of their love is turned back, their tender sympathies are withered, and their intellects dwarfed; just as vines are kept from struggling upward by weights laid upon them, and at length, by long continued pressure, run along the ground and climb no higher.

When books are opened and the general routine of lessons entered upon, there is still greater need for the young student to give voice to the thoughts within him. In this way he will gradually acquire fluency of speech, with an easy grace of manner that can never be won if the opportunity is now lost. Exercise rounds the muscles of the arm, and gives it beauty as well as strength. If we would have our children reap the highest advantage from study, we must accustom them to talk freely of what they study. In this manner memory will strengthen, judgment improve, taste become refined, and intellect be stimulated; while the organs of speech will become facile, easily ringing out the thoughts with proper inflections, and changes of expression. The voice should be like an instrument of music, sweet, mellow, winning, in itself a power of inestimable value to the possessor.

A family linked by such ties is like a paradise, a garden of delight: the parents, with knowledge and experience, leading and guiding; the children obedient, graceful, loving, opening their nearts to the parents just as the buds develop under the genial rays of the sun.

This habit of social converse does not of necessity imply the highest order of intellect. Great intelligences scarcely fail to shout over common minds. We do not, as a general rule, choose friends on account of brilliant conversational powers; these are inestimable in an acquaintance, but might prove a drawback in a nearer relationship. Still, so much of conversational power we need to link and bind family ties in sweet, intelligent, daily intercourse. A simple English ballad, well sung, touches the heart with deeper emotions than the splendid arias and bravuras that inspire only wonder, or have a certain nameless fascination that holds the listener spell-bound, but fail to give birth to higher, nobler, purer feelings.

The charm of conversation is in a genial assimilation to those with whom we converse, an adaptation to their manner of thought, a way of seeming to possess only so much mind as the person we converse with, talking like an equal. This power is not entirely a natural gift; it is and may be cultivated by giving attention, seizing just those points of a subject with which others feel most at home, slipping into other people's way of thought, and investing their ideas in a dress agreeable to them. Such persons can afford to be modest, and are sure to win attention, because they know how to adapt themselves to the minds of others. It is this power that renders one charming, fascinating, irresistible—a talent well worth cultivating by both sexes, but especially by woman.

Another advantage is the real value of this talent to its possessor; the influence over others acquired through this channel—their insight and experience winning all with whom they have to do to unfold their most secret treasures of thought, and thus assisting them to build their mental structure higher and still higher.

The intercourse of mind is a mystery. Such free and graceful conversational power may not be ours, it may not belong to our children; but let us remember that it is in part a cultivated growth. If we do not attain it to perfection, we can attempt it, beginning with our children when youug, training their just budding ideas. Time will prove our work. Effort well directed is never lost.

XII.

Hospitality.

HOSPITALITY is not only a cardinal virtue, but it is a strong social bond, uniting families, neighborhoods, and communities, cementing and making firm the integral parts of the great social system. Man is constituted a social being, sympathy is needful to him as the air he breathes. It is like the sun, dispensing warmth; by it he is stimulated to exertion and nerved for danger; his energies are sustained, his sensibilities made tender, and his intellect acute and far-seeing. Isolate him, set him apart from his kind, and he becomes a changed being; the vital forces of his nature ebb and flow with a dull, ponderous stroke. The waves of feeling sweep over the cold gray sands of a cheerless existence; the intellect is dwarfed, the inner sanctuary of the heart dismantled, and the fire on its altar becomes cold and dead.

It is by reason of man's social nature that God "set the solitary in families." Knowing what was in the heart of man, he has made provision for our mental as well as for our spiritual needs. He charges his followers to be lovers of hospitality, entertaining strangers, as thereby some have "entertained angels unawares." It is one of the fundamental principles of the Christian religion, that it does away with caste, and breaks down social barriers. Each and all of the great human family stand before Him as miserable offenders. Of what importance in the sight of God are the petty differences of condition between Dives and Lazarus, queens and serving women, pampered ladies and unsightly beggars? It was not the ivory and gold, the hangings of purple and fine linen, the pomegranates and the precious stones; it was not the altar, but the sacrifice laid upon the altar, the spirit in which it was made, the purity of motive, the humble, contrite heart, that were precious in the sight of God.

By hospitality the apostle did not mean to enjoin simply the entertaining of personal friends; neither did he limit it to distribution to the saints. "Blessed be God, even the Father of mercies and the God of all comfort, who comforteth us in all our tribulation, that we may be able to comfort them which are in any trouble, by the comfort wherewith we ourselves are comforted of God." This is the secret of hospitality, that we may comfort others.

If hospitality is a virtue that we would see our children possessed of, we must cultivate it at home—opening our doors especially to those who stand in need of comfort or consolation, that we may comfort them according to the measure that we have received. Hearts are strangely alike, little kindnesses find the quickest avenues; the look of sympathy, the firm hand-clasp, the tender, genial word, these cost nothing, why do we withhold them? Children learn of us; they do as we do. If we neglect the poor, shutting the door upon them because they are abject and uncomely, so will they. If we look coldly upon the stranger, passing him by because he is a stranger, so will they. Poor and perhaps sinful he may be, yet why may we not open our doors to him, give him the shelter of a roof, talk with him, pray with him, tell him of Jesus? He is a stranger; yet why may we not take him by the hand? Though a stranger to us, he may not be a stranger to God; and if a stranger and an alien, yet the dear heavenly Father is still waiting to receive him. Is this not a fitting opportunity to whisper in his ear the name of Jesus? Do we "covet earnestly the best gifts" for our children? we must not fail to let them see how good and sweet a thing it is to be kindly considerate one of another, ready with the right word in the right place, letting our light so shine that the beauty of holiness will be revealed, and the world be attracted and won by it.

In cultivating a spirit of hospitality, as in the distribution of our goods, the blessing that follows more than repays us for the self-denial practised. The sensible presence of the Master is given to us, and the comforting words, "Whosoever shall give to drink unto one of these little ones, a cup of cold water in my name, shall in no wise lose his reward." Subject as we are to change, the rolling years sweeping away friends like leaves before the autumn winds, and the home comfort gathered in a lifetime swallowed by fire or shipwreck, what security have we that some adverse gale will not strip us of the accidentals that go to make so large a part of every life?

In view of these changes, it is fitting that we keep open doors, ready to share with those who have less. If no more than a cup of cold water, do not deny the children the privilege of bearing it in their own hands; do not deprive them of the blessedness of doing it for Christ's sake. Comforting others will only prove another means of making home happy. Conversant with the sorrow, pain, and suffering of others, our children will be more sympathetic, more efficient in all the emergencies of life. Some of the warmest friendships this world has ever known had their origin in a word spoken to a stranger.

Children are attracted to each other without stopping to adjust the social balance. On several occasions going and coming from school, Margaret had been helped out of serious difficulty by Jephthah Hull, a roving, capricious lad, whose reputation was in no wise enviable in the community. Margaret's sympathy was aroused. Jephthah, or Jeph as he was called, had not a wicked look. His figure was tall, straight, and muscular; his eyes of a changeable gray hue—at times tender, pleading, almost reproachful; then bright, resolute, fearless; his hair was thick and curling, and the proud curve of his lips denoted a character that needed careful development. With no home, Jeph lived by doing odd jobs at anything he could find, and from being rash and impetuous he won for himself the reputation of being the instigator, if not the actual agent, of all the mischief practised in the neighborhood.

One night as I was listening to Maude, I heard Margaret talking with her father about Jeph and his manner of life. "Wild and boisterous as the boy is," she said, "his voice is mild and his manners respectful."

"But he is the terror of the community," said her father.

"Only think, papa; Jeph never had a home; he does not even remember that he had a mother. In his babyhood he was thrust out to live as he could; flung round from one place to another, he has never had any teaching. He has never been to school, and still he can read and write correctly."

The child's heart was effectually roused. I saw it, and I knew that her father would not refuse her.

"And if I take him as you wish, what then?"

"I will teach him, papa, until he has learned the little that I know, and by that time something else will open for him."

"We will try," answered her father. And thus Jeph came to our house. His duties were light, to sweep the office, light the fires, and keep the grounds in order. Small duties, but requiring faithfulness. At first he would forget, play truant, and was not disposed to bear the least rebuke. Margaret was quick to understand the boy, and she never tired of his caprices; she taught him from books, and mingled with her instruction words that touched upon his daily habits. Ere long the boy's confidence was won; his better nature was awakened; he saw great possibilities even for him; life wore a new aspect; his mind opened to kindly influences, he began to show uncommon brilliancy. As Margaret had said, when she had taught him the little that she knew, a way opened for him to go forward. This same friendless boy is now a world-renowned author, an earnest, active, Christian man.

This is not an isolated case; there are many, like Margaret, ready to take the little outcasts by the hand. But not all are thus ready. As we look upon the myriad waifs floating around us, we shall not soil our hands if we, having empty rooms, give warmth and shelter to little ones for whom Christ died; little ones to be taught to live and work for Him.

Poor and destitute, Jesus takes them in his arms. So let us teach our children to love them with a tender, abiding love; not to be led by them into evil, but to be ourselves their leaders—up to the good Physician. Blessed privilege! to comfort as we ourselves are comforted—giving according to the measure that we have received, blest in ourselves and in our children by so doing.

Genial hospitality betrays itself in the easy grace of a casual meeting—the tones of the voice showing interest, the eye filled with a tender light, the manner showing a certain heartiness that exalts the receiver into an equal. Doubtless all know homes of this description, where there is an easy welcoming of guests, the parents being assisted by their children; and the aim of all is to interest their guest without the appearance of effort. A rare blessing to the young it is, to be privileged with the acquaintance of such a Christian family; for none but a Christian family could thus carry out the spirit of the gospel, gladly taking the wanderer by the hand, and saying, "Come thou with us, for we will do thee good."

What a resting-place for the aged is a household in which these tender home influences come to them as portraits of the home-gathering above, its rest, content, and enjoyment. Such precious reunions strengthen the bond of Christian brotherhood; their golden glow warms the heart of the impenitent, causing them to exclaim, Behold, how beautiful the fellowship of Christian hearts! The memory of little kindnesses clings to them, and at length brings them to Jesus. As Christian mothers, is not this the work given us to do? Should we not be ready at all times to minister unto any we can benefit, imparting as freely as we receive? our highest enjoyment to be found in serving Christ, our highest praise, "She hath done what she could."

XIII.

Dress.

FROM the beginning the costume of nations has been in keeping with their attainments in civilization, architecture, and the fine arts. In the nomadic life, wandering tribes, dwelling in tents, were satisfied with coats of skins, sandals, and loose mantles, leaving the body free to act with its all its strength and suppleness. The dress of that early day did not require numberless changes to denote the wealth of the possessor; flocks and herds were the chief criterion, and if many "changes of raiment" were demanded, they were in good part intended for presents, or as tokens of favor offered to guests.

As walled towns began to appear, more protection was sought in dress. Armor was brought into use, and a greater variety of garments; still, the make was exceedingly simple, and the limbs were unimpeded and free in their movements. Down through the centuries we find beauty habited in loose, flowing garments, falling lightly about the figure, with a profusion of ornaments—gold, silver, ivory, and precious stones. Anklets with small silver bells made music as the maidens danced, and their round arms bare to the shoulder, were bound with bracelets, in keeping with their wealth. Jewels were extensively worn by the nations in the apostles' time. Hence the injunction, "Whose adorning, let it not be that outward adorning of plaiting the hair and of wearing of gold, or of putting on of apparel; but let it be the hidden man of the heart, in that which is not corruptible, even the ornament of a meek and quiet spirit. . . . . For after this manner in the old time the holy women adorned themselves." "Not with broidered hair, or gold, or pearls, or costly array; but, which becometh women professing godliness, with good works."

The apostle has reference here to the customs of the heathen women. While from his general teaching we cannot accuse him of wishing to do away with a becoming style of dress, we see plainly that he desired to make dress secondary: "a meek and quiet spirit," with "good works" being more desirable than costly array and precious stones. Paul and Peter would have women professing godliness make it known by outward expression, as well as by "chaste conversation, coupled with fear."

It is sufficient for our purpose to note the dividing line between the Christian woman and the woman of the world. Passing down the successive ages from the apostle's time to our own, is the echo of the same voice, "not with broidered hair, or gold, or pearls, or costly array; but, which becometh women professing godliness, with good works." In the history of the Christian church there was never a time perhaps when there was greater necessity for each individual member to walk humbly and circumspectly before God. The fires of strange philosophies and false creeds are seen on every hill; infidelity thrusts its slimy head and sinuous glittering folds into our colleges and institutions of learning; and the popular mind, floating out on the sea of speculation, dares, with impious hand, thrust back the gates, and with curious, prying eyes, seeks to gain knowledge of the invisible and unrevealed.

Living in an age eminently progressive, the elements brought into subjection, the caverns of the great deep but whispering galleries, thought flashing in a moment round the world, the secrets of the earth laid open to the eye of man, is there not danger that in our pride we may drift away from the old landmarks, and from the safe anchorage, and be tossed about by vain imaginings and shallow ideas of new and strange systems yet to come to light and die. With the spirit of speculation abroad in the land, is there not danger, lest in seeking "the unknown good," we neglect the plain command, discarded because so plain, so easily understood?

Looking into the mirror of God's word we find that the way is straight and narrow, and that the commands given to mankind were given for all time. Consequently, a broad and unbridled license in thought and in deed is not becoming in those who profess to be guided by the word of God.

In every age dress has not only had much to do in the petty distinctions of caste, and in marking the different grades of society, but it has been considered one of the signs of the times, an exponent or mirror, reflecting the onward movement of the age. For those who profess godliness, moderation is enjoined. They must be "temperate in all things," in eating, and drinking, and dress; with nothing absurd or ascetic, but studying simplicity, neatness, and order—a costume that befits a temple on which purity and beauty are plainly inscribed. The apostle himself was not beyond thinking of these things. In his letter to Timothy, asking for the cloak that he left at Troas, we see that he must have been moved by the same wants and needs that have such influence over us. Such knowledge of the apostle's life and manner brings him nearer to us; our sympathies are with him, and we are not so much inclined to consider him as severe in his restrictions. Paul did not despise the things of this life; neither does he desire that we should. He only asks that we "use them as not abusing;" making them secondary and subservient, and thinking more of comfort and convenience than of display.

There is a peculiar charm in adaptation. If we live conscientiously, not lightly esteeming the things of this life, but still thinking more of another, into which we are liable to enter at any moment, surely we shall not be inclined to spend our strength on this that perishes with the using, absorbing time that is of inestimable value. If eternity is in reality the chief concern, we shall not wish to encumber ourselves or our children with needless care and anxiety. The traveller chooses his dress according to the season; it is adapted to his necessities, it is soiled and travel-stained perhaps. What difference? He will put on fresh apparel when he reaches his journey's end. He does not think of the way, in the anticipation of what is before him. Life is a journey; let our travelling dress be appropriate, plain, simple, unostentatious, but let our best robe be the white robe of our heavenly home.

In the natural world, where there are hidden and special gifts, outward show is often lacking. Singing birds wear the plainest plumage, and the sweetest flowers are the small, unpretending ones.

If fitness is needful in the selection of garments, fitness is likewise requisite in the wearing. A style of dress pretty and becoming at home, may not be suitable for church. A pretty and becoming dress for a breakfast or a dinner party, is not always the one in which we should enter the street cars, or make a long journey. Neither are we to habit ourselves in evening costume when we visit the sick, or call on the poor and the necessitous. As Christians, we should show a due regard to fitness in this respect, selecting for ourselves and for our children according to time and place, with a wise adaptation in all that we do.

Returning from school on one occasion, Maude came rushing into my room, the blue eyes earnest and pleading, the face bright and arch, as the child danced up before me with a card of invitation in her hand. "Mamma, Lucy Fan wants me to come to her party, Thursday. Can I go, please?"

Mr. and Mrs. Fan were members of a sister church. I knew them slightly, and knew that the children were pleasant and agreeable in manner. I saw nothing against it, and willing to give the child pleasure, gave my assent. It was our habit to dress prettily and neatly at home, and when we went out we aimed at nothing more. On this occasion, I made for Maude a simple dress of white swiss, with a blue sash for the waist. It was a trifle prettier than usual, and when the day came and Maude was dressed, her soft brown hair falling in ringlets over her plump shoulders, her eyes sparkling and her cheeks rosy with health, I must confess to a little pride and an extra kiss. Papa kissed the child: "I hope my little girl will enjoy herself very much." Then turning, he once more kissed the ruddy cheek, and said, "May the heart of my little girl be as pure as her dress."

Jem was proud of his sister. I saw it as he walked down the street, and I fear my own heart was full of pride. Maude looked so sweet and good, and I was sure that all would appreciate the innocent beauty of my child.

At night her father brought her home; and as I caught a glimpse of the white face, I saw that Maude was sadly tried.

"What is it, pet?" said I, as I folded her in my arms.

"O mamma!" and the tears were streaming down her cheeks. I saw the child was grieved, and did not urge her. It was a long time before she could tell me, and then only in broken snatches, that it was the simplicity of her dress, Lucy's friends taking exception to one so plainly dressed.

"Why, what was your mother thinking of? Did she know it was to be a dress party?" cried one.

"I never wear anything but white," stammered Maude.

"A regular little nun. But why did you not have ruffles, or flounces of Valenciennes?"

"Mamma thinks plain dresses are the prettiest."

"Why, where has she lived? Nobody thinks of wearing a plain dress; it makes you look like a little Methodist."

"I was afraid it would be so," and Margaret crept up to Maude and tried to comfort her.

"What led you to think so?" I asked.

"At Miss Bernard's, where Lucy goes to school, there is a great display of dress. Sarah Erskine says the girls are in party costume all the time."

There is a fascination in gay dress,

an invisible influence, wrapping one in folds too strong to be broken by weak hands. Fortune is a fickle goddess; her favors are seldom dispensed to the same family for two centuries; and if it were otherwise, and if one can afford to dress richly, is the school-room a place to exhibit finery? Here the daughters of the poor and the rich meet for the purpose of mental improvement, preparing for the duties and responsibilities of social life; study is the duty of each, and promotion should depend upon merit alone. A great blemish it must be for pupils in the same class, sitting on the same seats, occupying the same rooms, to show a marked disparity in dress and appearance. Pride is inherent, and the love of dress natural to woman. Much of the sin in after years, the murmuring and repining, has had its origin in the undue display of dress in the school-room. The daughter of the rich man priding herself on the magnificence of her wardrobe; the daughter of the poor man, a heavy tax to her parents, and then dissatisfied, forgetful of her opportunities, thinking only of display, and at length resorting to unhallowed means to gratify her passion for dress.

The time to instil right principles is in childhood. Knowing the heart of our daughters, cannot we teach them that the mind is more than the body, the heart more than the mind? Cannot we teach them that youth is never so attractive as when dressed simply? Cannot we make it plain to them that beauty is enhanced by it, just as the diamond shows to the greatest advantage when set simply? Cannot we teach them the beauty of adaptation, enjoining upon them the necessity of a proper influence, that a modest dress is becoming in public assemblies, and that greater care is needful in color, make, and finish, for wear in a promiscuous throng. Cannot we show them that display is to be avoided in church? that simplicity, good taste, and neatness are indispensable for God's house? As worshippers, we go up to his courts; as suppliants, we lay our offering upon the altar, conscious that the eye of the Most High looketh at the heart, and not on the outward adorning.

In church, as in school, the rich and the poor meet together. Have we the right to dress so that a weak brother or sister shall be offended? The eye is pained and the heart is distressed by little things.

An indiscriminate display of jewelry is quite offensive to good taste. True, there are those who think it incumbent upon them to wear all that they have upon every occasion. At breakfast, we see them with fingers loaded with rings, pendants in their ears, ornamental combs, with hair perhaps in curl papers. A pretty chintz wrapper, with hair neatly arranged, and without jewels, would form a charming contrast to such an appearance.

Inappropriateness of dress belongs more especially to us as a people than to any other nation. The English woman, in travelling, provides herself with coarse, strong garments, and discards jewelry. The advantages of fine dress are reserved for the drawing-room. The good Victoria goes to Scotland to enjoy herself. Her costume is plain and simple, and in the small church at Balmoral there is nothing of display to attract the eye, or to distract the heart of the humblest worshipper.

A little sober thought upon this question will be enough to convince the most inconsistent. A more careful style of dress at home, with less expense and less display abroad, would tend more to the happiness of families, than volumes of theories, discussion, and even legislation. Love has need to be very strong indeed, that can stand tamely and contrast the negligent appearance of the morning dress with the elaborate style and elegant decorations put on to please the eyes of strangers. A fresh, charming costume goes far towards making a happy home. As well might we expect a bird to sing, with her plumage covered with mud, as a woman to be cheerful and amiable in a soiled, neglected costume.

Another peculiarity, and one which we would in no wise overlook, is the disparity of dress between mother and daughter: the jewels and beautiful garments worn by the latter, the self-denial and economy practised by the former. The reverse would seem more in keeping; the ravages of time render necessary some advantage of dress; the comeliness of youth is sufficient without the aid of rich materials and costly ornaments.

A few weeks since, I attended commencement exercises at a girls' school. The class of graduates was large; they were fine, healthy-looking girls, all habited in white of different materials and fashions. One of them wore a white moiré, with an exceedingly short skirt, "so that she might look more youthful." Her mother was sitting near her in a plain dress, without ornament of any kind. I could not but think how still more youthful and lovely the daughter would have looked in a simple white swiss, falling gracefully about her, leaving the rich, stiff moiré for her mother.

In cultivating the minds of our daughters we are surely not to leave to the last a subject on which so much depends. If we instil into their minds while children the proper regard for dress, we may hope that in youth they will not be inclined to run into excesses, but will study what is becoming, and wear it in no spirit of ostentation, but to render home more attractive. God has dressed the flowers in beauty, and he has no desire that we should be unmindful of ourselves.

"Know ye not that ye are the temple of God?" A temple is built expressly with an end in view—the indwelling of God; the architecture is appropriate, the beams are laid in strength, and the altar and the hangings in keeping with the idea of worship. Thus with the temple of the Holy Spirit, set apart and kept with the same end in view; the heart an altar on which sacrifice is laid, the ornament of a meek and quiet spirit woven in the hangings of the sanctuary; the whole adapted to inspire good and pure thoughts, and lead the careless and indifferent to see and acknowledge the blessedness of those who love and honor God.

XIV.

Amusements.

AS our daughters grew older, there were decisions to make, entertainments to enjoy, and assemblies to shun; rendering it necessary for us to ask still oftener for direction and guidance, lest we should fail to do according to His will. Jem likewise had his associates; and as Gertrude was still warmly attached to Margaret, it is possible that we had more visitors by reason of juxtaposition to the large house over the way. It was the last year with Margaret at school, and try as I would, I could not keep the shadow from my heart. I knew these small gatherings were but a foretaste of what there was in store. Society had claims and would be sure to assert them. My child was slipping from me. Not that her love was less, or her confidences diminished; but the sweet placid beauty of her face was attractive, her manner cordial, and her words so gentle that the poorest and most timid of her acquaintances were not repelled.

As I before said, music was cultivated by us, not as an accomplishment, but as a necessity. It entered into our being, was a part of our life; our daily worship was not complete without it. From her infancy Margaret had shown a rare talent for it, her voice was flexible and sweet, and she had a peculiar power of expression. It was the effect of culture, bringing out the native capacity, and so perfectly that there was seemingly nothing of art about it: the song being only the avenue to convey the sentiment, the thought floating out on the wings of melody filling the ear with delight.

She might have played as well perhaps, but loving books, she did not think best to take the time, neither did we encourage her learning more of music than was needful to make home happy, and enable her to sing in the sanctuary and in the prayer-meeting, leaving brilliant execution and a finished touch to amateurs and professors.

Many families consider music in the same category as dancing, or believe that the cultivation of one, leads to the cultivation and love of the other. Never was a greater mistake. True, dancing is usually accompanied by music, the steps in keeping with the musical measure, but it is a music that invites to physical action without touching the loftier emotions of the soul. As a physical exercise dancing may have its advantages, but is it in itself calculated to advance the intellectual or the spiritual well-being of our children? Will our sons be better fitted to take their places in the arena of life? Will their integrity be the brighter for their being adepts in the ball-room? Will our daughters be more attractive in the home circle? Will their qualities of heart and mind mature more thoroughly in such an atmosphere? Will the friends they make, the acquaintances they form in the quadrille and the waltz prove desirable as lifelong companions? If not, can we trust them there?

"But a public dance is altogether different from a quiet cotillon in the parlor." True, there is not the crowd. But what is the difference between taking a glass of brandy at one's sideboard, or taking it in the saloon? the brandy is the same, the poison acts in the same manner; it does not change the nature of the beverage, or lessen the evil, that it is private.

Dancing is in itself fascinating, the meeting of the sexes in the dance thrills the frame with the same impulse in the parlor as in the public assembly. If one is wrong, surely the other cannot be defended, for both are the same, save in extent. Poison taken into the system in a large dose, produces instant death; a small quantity works more slowly, but leads to the same result. That there are Christian parents who view this differently I am aware; parents who dress their daughters for the social dance, while they themselves go to the prayer-meeting. I have known such, we have all known them perhaps. But I do not know parents of this kind whose hearts are cheered by seeing their children brought to Christ; the arrangement is not one that favors early piety. We should not expect to see a Timothy, a Samuel, a Daniel, or a Mary in such a house. "As for me and my house, we will serve the Lord," would seem the natural motto of parents who profess to put their confidence in God. If we love an object it is our first thought how we may please the object of our love. The impenitent do not love God; hence they do not desire to please him; the thought of God is not in their hearts. The believer professes to love him, but love is shown by obedience. If we love him, we shall keep his commandments. Is there a line in the Bible that goes to prove that the giddy whirl of the waltz is not at all objectionable if indulged in quietly, and still is averse to purity and good morals if indulged in for a longer period, or in a public assembly?

"And whatsoever ye do in word or deed, do all in the name of the Lord Jesus." "Abstain from all appearance of evil." If these requirements have any weight, can the inmates of a godly household give themselves to an amusement upon which, from its very nature, they could not ask the blessing of God?

But I hear it said, "There is no standard with reference to this; we are each at liberty to follow the dictates of our own conscience; and as for our children, if they think it is wrong when they are older, it will be for them to abstain from it." But our children were given us to bring up for God. If their lives prove a failure, will he not require a reason? If our children are finally lost, shall we not be in a measure responsible? Children were not given to lead the parents; but to be led, guided, taught by the parents. A fearful charge. Can we afford to run the risk of letting them dance and waltz into eternity? Can we stand idly by, saying to each other, "When they are older, they will do different, youth is the time for enjoyment, we will not mar their pleasure, neither will we thwart their inclinations?" Have we any surety of their lives? Because we have them to-day, have we any pledge that they will be ours to-morrow? They are slipping away from us; now is the time to lay foundations, to instil right principles; the opportunity once lost can never be regained. If we wish to see our sons walking in the path of truth: if we desire to see our daughters as "corner-stones polished after the similitude of a palace," we must watch over them closely; seeking their happiness in all healthful ways, and abstaining conscientiously from those diversions, which, however harmless they may seem, add nothing to intellectual culture and true spiritual growth, and are ruled simply by the god of this world.

Next to dancing, private theatricals are defended by many parents. But why private? If the stage is to be commended, why not go publicly? "The theatre is not just the place for children," says one; "there are so many other things included, that it is now almost impossible to see a good play." And why is this? Simply that the class who frequent the theatre desire something more than the representation of the play. The managers of the theatre say freely that they could not keep it up if not for the objectionable features of the drama. The very best plays of Shakespeare, set off with the best acting, and heightened by exquisite scenery, to use the ordinary phraseology, do not "pay." No wonder that the theatre is not just the place for children. The only wonder is that any parent should think of it for a moment in connection with his children.

True, private theatricals might be free from some of these objections. But to what profit? An intelligent reading of Shakespeare would give one as good an idea of character. I recollect listening to one of our best tragedians as he read Macbeth; quite as instructive, he allowed, as it would have been on the boards: a little imagination could easily construct a scaffolding, with scenery and all the et ceteras of stage exhibition; and with this exception, the rendering was the same.

The minds of the young are like some deftly strung instrument, the softest touch makes an impression, and the song evoked adds to the beauty or to the deformity of the finished work. A merely sensuous delight, a picture, or a wave of melody may please the eye or charm the ear with its sweetness, and still fail to touch the heart. If the mind is more than the body, and the heart more than the mind, then time that is spent for other than the highest good must be time misspent. Life is not to be frittered away without profit. Eternity is too near and too enduring to be unthought of and unprovided for.

As in childhood we are careful to provide for the health and well-being of our children, permitting them to enjoy all healthy exercise, and plays well fitted to give tone to their muscles and strength to their constitution, so in youth we should make an effort to secure such amusements as will cause the full development of their mental faculties and conduce to their greatest vigor through life.

To converse well requires study and practice. Home can hardly be called happy without the intelligent exercise of the organs of speech; commonplace platitudes pall on the ear, and with nothing to interest them at home, the inmates of our dwellings will seek places that promise them more in this respect. To read well is an accomplishment of immense value in the home circle. What can be a more beautiful picture than the evening gatherings in a well-appointed home: the old and the young, with sewing, books, and music, seasoned with the wisdom of age, the gay sparkle of youth, and the prattle of little children. The atmosphere of such a home is favorable to the purity of body and soul. Happiness is a plant of daily growth, and culture is built up of opportunities. Outward circumstances have little to do with inward content; the life we lead is the effect of the atmosphere we breathe in our homes.

Musical soirees have an effect highly desirable. Some of the finest minds the world has ever known have been in the habit of meeting one evening in every week for the purpose of mental improvement and enjoyment, giving full scope to their powers of speech, with criticisms and discussions on scientific subjects and the questions of the day—repartee and brilliant bon-mots stimulating and engaging and strengthening the faculties. Lectures and debates, chemical experiments and scientific disquisitions give a pleasing variety and intelligent entertainment to the mind.

Looking at life as a sphere of duty, we cannot consider a mere idle diversion which has no higher aim than to kill time, as entering into the life-plan. Yet effort of every kind needs intervals of relaxation—some agreeable change relaxing thought, and giving the jaded powers of mind and body time to regain elasticity and vigor. The young especially need this. But what mother will be satisfied to give her children husks, when it is in her power to provide them wholesome food? Thus with amusement. What mother will be willing to let her daughter spend the time unwisely, when it is in her power to provide more suitable entertainment?

There is too prevalent in our day a certain clanship, a division and subdivision of society, people associating together exclusively according to age and social fellowship; but there cannot be a greater mistake as far as improvement is concerned, and there must be a serious loss of the enjoyment arising from the pleasing interchange of thought and feeling. Beauty and homeliness, youth and age, the learned and the ignorant, make up God's world. Variety is needful. We do not see the gardener filling all his beds with the same flowers; beautiful as they may be, the monotony would cease to give pleasure; delicious as their perfume might be, we should sigh for some variety of fragrance. In our social gatherings why should we confine ourselves to the range of a certain moneyed rank, or of a certain intellectual calibre? Social meetings are for relaxation, for entertainment; study is laid aside, thought unbends itself, the man of science looks for diversion; the lady of brilliant conversational powers finds a listener in some silent but appreciative friend. It is not wise to be too exclusive, neither is it wise to bring up our children to feel that there is no enjoyment outside a prescribed circle of age or of position. A long list of acquaintances adds to our personal happiness, helps to deepen the channel of our ideas, and to enlarge the scope of our benevolent feelings. Broad views of men and things can only be gained in this way; prejudice, bigotry, and all uncharitableness are thus thrust out, and a genial well-bred manner acquired.

Teaching our children to be kind and considerate, we are also to tone down their eager expectancy. Every acquaintance is not likely to turn into a friend. To be attracted by people, to meet them at stated intervals, to be cordial and friendly in no wise requires undue confidence towards all. A pleasing exterior, good manners and correct deportment constitute an agreeable acquaintance. But a friend is one to whom we are drawn by a certain congeniality of soul, with a thrilling pleasure when we meet, a sympathetic, harmonious blending of two natures, and the deep satisfaction of feeling that each is understood, appreciated, valued for choice gifts and close intimacies unknown to the world. Acquaintances are counted by scores; friends are few as angel visitors. It is a rare life that finds more that one, genuine and lasting; many go on to the grave with less.

We do not aim by this to teach our children that it is impossible for an acquaintance to become a valued friend; but only to save them from impatience and repining because the new acquaintance does not prove to be all that they thought to find. Until experience has taught a lesson, there is something intolerable to youth in realizing the slight tenure which they have on all they see; the little claim they have or are really likely to have on society around them. To teach them to be contented with the refreshment and solace they can gain from good society, is to do them a lasting service, and the lesson can be taught by no one so well as by the mother. She also can teach them that there are real and substantial qualities which render an acquaintance charming, that would be insufficient in a friend; brilliancy of thought, fluency of speech, vivacity and an easy grace of manner fascinate us in society; but these may be united with some alloy that would be fatal to the closer bond of friendship. A knowledge of this will aid both our sons and our daughters in the choice they make of friends; and thus mistakes will be prevented that, if once made, can never be rectified. A pleasant acquaintance can be found in a day, in an hour perhaps; but a friend is chosen, not for external qualities, but for innate principles of heart and mind, the beauty of which will increase, the more intimate the union.

Another lesson that will be of essential service to our children is to give them to see plainly, that society requires great powers of reticence and self-control in those who mix in it. It is so natural for the inexperienced to commit themselves by over energy of expression, by over-earnest tones, in a word, by exposing their hidden life at inappropriate times and places; and on becoming conscious of it they are mortified, and their self-respect receives a wound. Every person accustomed to society understands that he must not obtrude his honest convictions too forcibly. The light, passing superficial treatment of a subject does not imply that people have not convictions which elsewhere, in the privacy of home, or when duty requires, they can express with warmth and force; but experience has taught them that the unrestrained liberty of speech of one, would be to the hinderance of others.

Thus we have touched upon several social questions, as having an intimate relation with amusements or relaxation in the ordinary acceptation of the word. For social beings, amusement would cease to be amusement if taken in solitude; while in most cases the choice of amusement depends not a little upon the choice of friends. "Show me a man's friends, and I can tell you what kind of a man he is, and the places that he loves to frequent."

It becomes us to choose wisely for our children with reference to their amusements, as well as to their friends. It is not the great events of life, but rather the little daily acts that show character: the hours of recreation may be like the light breeze that fills our sails and sends us onward with a smooth gliding motion; or they may become like the hot breath from the desert withering and destroying all the verdure that lies in its pathway.

XV.

Domestic Relations.

IT is frequently said, and I once felt, that the happiest period in a mother's life was with her little ones in her arms; the patter of their tiny feet making music all day long, their gleeful voices merry as robins in spring-time, and their eyes like unfathomed wells in which great and wonderful truths are to be mirrored. But now, as I sit with such a sweet restful feeling, listening to Margaret singing at her work, I am inclined to think the happiness the mother feels in nursing her babes is less than the sweet joy that floods her heart when those dear babes are spared to reach their youth. The fresh-blown flower is sweeter than the bud; the bird that sings a strong clear note is more prized than when a helpless thing it chirped and fluttered, waiting for its wings. My birds are fledged; and I 'm half afraid they 'll leave me all too soon.

Through school, but not through study, Margaret still has her lessons, and Maude has her studious hours, but we are together just as in the old days. Our home is still the same. The sunshine slants across the roof of the large house over the way and upon ours just as it used to do. Papa is now in riper years, but Margaret and Maude go to meet him as they used to; Jem is in college, Gertrude comes through the wicker gate, and with the sunshine on her rippling curls, we cross the meadow, hunting cowslips and ladyslippers. Sometimes in sportive mood Maude hides her head and laughs a little gleeful laugh to cheat me with the thought of years ago; and Margaret fills her hand with flowers, with a look of love and reverence up to Him who of his boundless mercy made this world so beautiful.

Companions more than children, sharers of thought, co-laborers, 'tis sweet to hear them talk of views and feelings such as we knew of old. They have a kind of second youth more lovely than the first; the current of their being is stirred with every shadow on the grass, the rippling river and the bird-notes calling up sweet echoes in their hearts. There are lessons not found in books, read by those who know the alphabet of God's love; music, not written by the pen of man, and pictures more grand and beautiful than ever painter drew. The wonders of God's world are dimly understood at best, and those that love him not are blinder than the moles, not to see and recognize his hand. The natural heart looks through distorted eyes, and only flaunting scenes and gaudy colors please. God is revealed by little things; hence children draw the nearest, spelling out his words of love, saying them over and again for fear they will forget. What a pity that we are not always children, loving and trusting; ready to sleep and eat and enjoy without that anxious forethought that tries to shoulder all in spite of what He says, "Come, follow me; come close; lean hard." The child, half unconscious, goes to Him; while we, knowing our guilt, hang back.

Gertrude has found some pebbles on the shore, and to her eyes they have a strange significance. Years ago, a barefooted, blue-eyed child, she played and gathered pebbles on these very sands, while her grandmother, with white hair and faltering steps was near her, saying, "God has been good, is always good;" and then added, as she slipped her arm in mine, "could I only know that the departed shall look down from his presence and see his promises all fulfilled." I remember the last sad day of her life, and how, when I cried as though my heart would break, my mother bade me bring the Book, and with her trembling fingers turned the leaves and pointed me to these words:

"Lord, thou hast been our dwelling-place in all generations. Before the mountains were brought forth, or ever thou hadst formed the earth and the world, even from everlasting to everlasting, thou art God. The days of our years are threescore years and ten; and if by reason of strength they be fourscore years, yet is their strength labor and sorrow: for it is soon cut off, and we fly away. Make us glad according to the days wherein thou hast afflicted us, and the years wherein we have seen evil. And let the beauty of the Lord our God be upon us: and establish thou the work of our hands upon us; yea, the work of our hands establish thou it."

"God has been good to me," I said, as the golden head of my child rested on my shoulder; "God has been good to me!" and the birds trilled it from bough to bough, and the flowers rang out a silvery chime. It was the vesper hour, and nature, glad and happy, swelled out the glorious anthem, "Praise ye the Lord!"

The sun sinks slowly, while waves of opal light stream over the meadow, and fall with a benediction on the distant hills. The flowers begin to fold their leaves, and the birds are flying homeward. Gertrude's arm is twined around Margaret, and the blue eyes are filled with a wealth of love. Maude is leaning on my arm, not now clinging to my fingers, as in that olden time. It does not seem so very long ago; and the eyes that look into mine are little changed. Humble as our path is, it has been full of mercy.

"Papa is coming!" and away springs Maude. There's a merry chase down the path and over the stile. Papa's step is almost as fleet as when he raced with Jem. We miss the boy. I cannot make his loss real. It seems but yesterday that his head was pillowed on my arm, his rosy face nestling in my bosom. What a privilege it is to lead these babes up through the years to maturity, a work of which we can be justly proud; and very humble too, for scarcely could we do it, but for the fellowship of Mary's Son, a babe like ours, once nourished and petted in the same way. 'T is sweet to be the mother of a son whom we can teach to follow in His steps.

Silvery waves of light have chased the gold away, and our home temple, overrun with vines, is curtained in with purple. It is new for papa to place me in the chair. At first I declined it: "Rest is not for me." "But the girls," he said, "will never learn to keep house unless they once begin. There never can be a better time than when they come home from school, and with their mother's eyes keen to detect mistakes; her patience and sweet encouragement; her experience a well of wisdom, from which they are to draw needful supplies."

"Come, mother, tea is ready!" and I find myself a guest. Margaret is in the chair behind the urn. It is pleasant, and still I am half afraid I shall grow to love this leisure, and thus miss something left for me to do. Papa seems not afraid; and the plate of biscuit, white and light as foam, wins praise from all. Maude begs me to see if her quinces are as nice as mine last year. "Better, if I remember aright," I said; and her blue eyes dance with joy. "I was afraid I might have made some mistake."

"Experiments may sometimes fail, and yet give no ground for discouragement," says papa, and goes on to show that mistakes may sometimes profit more than uniform success. We grow careless and forget when all is fair; but when we fail once and again, then comes the effort. More and more we strive and learn, and at last stand where we aimed to stand, but where we never should have stood had failure not been written on our first efforts.

High on the list of woman's choicest gifts is to be the keeper of a well-ordered house. How much we lose by undervaluing it—some from necessity, and others still through choice, neglecting the little things that go to make a home, and are only done through love. Which of us but remembers the mother's loaf and fragrant cup of tea, the table with a cloth of spotless white, the china cups and plates with rim of gold, the carpet covered with a cloth to catch the children's crumbs, the windows shaded just enough to give a pleasant light. The richest feasts are only found where love abides.

I remember such a home; and with her head upon my knees Maude listens as I tell her of the bread kneaded long and well, the oven brought to a white heat, and the clock at hand to mark the time.

"Your bread was good, of course," was naively said.

"Heavy as lead!" I replied; and my heart goes back to that first loaf. "Gladly would I have then given the little fund of learning I possessed for so much knowledge as was needed to make bread."

"Did you try again?"

"Once more, and failed."

"And then?"

"I thought of a poor woman living in a rich man's house, and going to her, asked for what I should have learned before.

"'There 's nothing easier,' she kindly said. 'I 'll show you once, and after that it will come easy. People that want to do, can do; and those that do n't, can't.'

"It was only another way of saying that woman's work is best done through love—a cheerful, happy service, just as the sun shines. A small thing it may seem to have a pleasant room, and a tidy well-kept house; but it is not small in its effects: home pictures stamped upon the heart cling there through life. If we would be to our daughters all that mothers should be, we must teach them how to order households. It is not enough for them to sit by and look on; they must bear the burden, studying out for themselves, and improving on our plans. There is nothing stationary in this world of ours; and even the science of cooking does not stand still.

Besides the dishes suited to our taste, and the nameless comforts which help to hold hearts that might otherwise go astray, our daughters are to learn a proper deportment toward dependants; to deal with them not only justly, but kindly. With an experimental knowledge of the service required, they will know how to arrange so that it may be easier to perform, and more acceptably rendered. Such knowledge comes not by chance. As well might we sit with folded hands in our attempt to read a new language, or to unravel problems in geometry. Nothing is accomplished without labor; and there never was a successful housekeeper, neither can there be, who does not make her home duties a study. The tastes of her husband, the inclinations of her children, the tendencies of her domestics, must all be well understood and cared for. If she would have a happy home, she must make it so.

But some one is ready to say, "It is unjust to make woman so responsible." As well find fault with the mainspring in a watch, the keynote in music, the intricacies of a machine that sets all the rest in motion. The mother does not of necessity do all. Each member of a household is responsible in a degree for the happiness and the well-being of the family. But is not the mother the centre around which all the others cluster? Let sickness lay its hand upon her, and gloom settles over the dwelling; and should death come, too late we learn our dependence upon a mother.

In view of future probabilities, should we not aim to educate our daughters to understand practically the minutiæ of social and domestic life? Should we not accustom them to bear a measure of responsibility from their earliest childhood? Then, if changes come, and come they will, they will be prepared to stand in their lot. What more lovely, what more noble than to see a daughter stepping into the vacant place, the comfort, the support of her father; the guide, the adviser, the patient, devoted friend to younger brothers and sisters? All over our land there are such daughters. God's choicest blessings rest upon them; his arm is theirs to lean upon. True, they may not know here the good they do, but they shall reap in due time a large reward.

Again, there are those who are not of this stamp; those who seek their own rather than another's good; vain, idle, pleasure-loving, impatient of rebuke, and not given to learn. Have we not as mothers something to do in this matter? Cannot we turn the tide in our own households? Cannot we teach a more acceptable way?

A few years since I enjoyed the intimate acquaintance of two families; both of them Christian households, both blessed with lovely daughters, both in circumstances of plenty and prosperity, both frequenting the same church; but how unlike in the whole internal order and harmony of domestic life.

The mother of one family sat as a queen in the midst of loving subjects; everything in her kingdom was amenable to law, the law of kindness and love. Order was in all her realm, and over all she presided with an unaffected grace, a charming self-poised manner, that won the love and admiration of all who enjoyed her acquaintance.

The other was a woman who loved her children not wisely. In their infancy she could not bear to cross them. Reading her Bible, she neglected that portion of it which says, "Chasten thy son while there is hope, and let not thy soul spare for his crying." Sitting at her ease, she flattered herself that, when they were older, they would turn of themselves. Does the wild horse tame himself? Does he yield his will without the bit? Too late this mother saw her mistake. The temper, inclination, and passion she could once have swayed, grew with years to be strong, wayward, and unmanageable. Anarchy, confusion, and hatred were in her house; sorrow was in her heart.

Is it wrong to think that, with the same careful training, the happiness of the last-named family would have equalled that of the first? Had the influence of the mothers been the same, the teaching alike, would not the result have been the same? If not, why do we find in the inspired volume so much said with reference to bringing up a child in the way that he should go? and why do we see the righteous indignation of God poured out upon those who refuse to obey him in this respect? Eli was condemned because he restrained not his children. "My son, keep thy father's commandment, and forsake not the law of thy mother." There must be a commandment and a law in every household.

God's favor is for the obedient. If we would see our children honorable in the earth, we must restrain and guide them in their infancy. If we would see them endowed plenteously with the spirit of divine grace, we must teach them to love God's service. Responsible as are the duties, arduous as are the cares that centre around the mother, if we but undertake them with a humble dependence on God, a cheerful, teachable spirit, leaning upon him, we shall succeed.

XVI.

Woman's Work in the Church.

THUS far we have spoken of woman's work in the social and domestic circle; a work that, however important in itself, radiates outward. Concentrate as we may the sun's rays, we cannot confine them. The atmosphere is warmed by them, the earth is invigorated, vegetation is rendered beautiful. Wherever they go, into the home of the millionaire, or into the hovel of the day-laborer, brightness goes with them. Woman's influence in her own home, although concentrated, is not confined there. Like the sunlight, it goes out into the community in which she dwells; goes with a blessing, genial, winning, constraining; or cold, formal, withering. But it is premised that we are talking with Christian mothers; mothers who aim to bring up their children and to order their households in the fear of the Lord; mothers whose little ones, like our own, are strong in stature, willing to share the burden, dividing the labor of the household, and using the time so that a reasonable share of leisure is the result.

Living in an age when the question of woman's position in the church is so often asked, it becomes us to pause and reflect, bringing knowledge and judgment to our aid, unfettered by prejudice, and only guided by the word of God. In the sacred volume we find unmistakable evidence that woman's graces blossom into the greatest beauty in the atmosphere of her own home; that her crowning grace is to be a mother, intrusted with the culture of immortal souls. We have aimed only to show the strength of woman's influence in the family; but who of us will not readily admit the influence of one who has the ability and the tact of leadership in the transforming of neighborhoods and communities? Look as her admirers hang upon her words. Her opinions are law, her wishes commands. Her manner, dress, style, conversation, are imitated by many around her. Why is this? Simply that she is charming as a woman, and womanly in all her ways. Would you learn the spell? It is in forgetfulness of self, and an artless ease that carries with it the charm of unconsciousness.

This transforming influence of woman, exerted first of all in her own home—winning her husband, her children, her domestics by the charm of her conversation, the admirable arrangement of her household, the wisdom displayed in all her ways—such influence is the effect of study, of forethought, and of plan. To admit this is not to lessen respect for woman's modest simplicity, or to take an iota from faith in her integrity. As a woman, God has endowed her with attractive qualities. He has given her beauty and a winning grace. Why was this, but that she should win by it love and esteem? It is her nature: love is the atmosphere in which she lives, thinks, and feels; it is the stimulant to exertion, the awakener of genius, the groundwork of all that is high and noble in her being.

The minister studies, that he may explain and make clear to the minds of men the grand theme on which he is to speak; the orator studies to fascinate and to hold in thrall the judgment of his listeners; the painter studies to charm by his lifelike representation; the sculptor studies to throw life into the block of senseless marble: and should not woman study to win by her life, to charm by her speech, to reflect in all her ways the graces of a pure, noble Christian womanhood?

Clearly as her position is defined in the family, it does not appear so exactly defined in church work; and wisely, for were there definite and specific rules, they might lead to usages in themselves inimical to the true interests of the church. All that we can now gather is to do good as we have opportunity; the woman with a family and the woman without, each doing what she can. It is too generally true that the great body of Christian women have felt that they had little to do but to listen; the younger ones perhaps to take charge of classes in the Sabbath-school, with an occasional call or distribution of tracts among the poor. leaving the great bulk of the work of the church to the pastor and officers. A new era has dawned; gleams of light from the primitive church point to a more general use of woman's tact and talent. The voice of the apostle Paul is heard in commendation of sister laborers, and the question is asked, What more can be done by woman in our churches?

Far be it from me to presume to define the exact position of woman, or any body of women, in the church of Christ. Neither can I see that any definite plan for all can be established. We must leave it for each individual to use her time wisely, conscious that for the use as for the abuse of it, she is to give account. God has specified certain things, making them clear, distinct, and unchangeable. There are others that he has left, not limiting the performance to any definite agency. We are told to pray; and while it would seem a fitting posture for suppliants to kneel, there is no doubt but equally acceptable prayer may be offered in any other preferred posture of the body. It is not the posture, but the spirit, that renders prayer acceptable.

The word of God is unchangeable. His commands are as binding to-day as in the apostles' time; but upon minor points the ways and means may change. Church architecture is not the same as in primitive times, the manner of worship is not in all respects what it was then; but the spirit of worship, the love, zeal, faith, earnestness to follow Christ, are the same. Neither do we presume to dictate as to the appointment of deaconesses. That they have been productive of good there can be no doubt; training women for religious service just as we train them for teachers and for nurses.

For this position only women of the requisite age and experience are eligible. The mother of a family should not be expected to leave her duties; the young and beautiful girl should be excused for reasons quite as obvious.

Work for Christ is broad and comprehensive. We would not lay a feather's weight upon the conscience of one faithfully striving to work for Jesus; neither can we say this is the way, or that is the way. Circumstances of life vary. Culture, custom, and experience are unlike in different localities. God has not set all women in families. From many he has taken away the delight of their eyes, the idol of their souls, stripped them of all and everything to which they could turn for support, for sympathy, for love. And why? There is a reason for all this. God doth not willingly afflict. His compassionate heart is moved by our tears; our sorrow is his sorrow. In removing those on whom we leaned he shows plainly that he would have us lean upon him. In depriving us of the work that we had thought our own, he says plainly that he has something else for us to do—something that will better serve the interests of the Redeemer's kingdom.

A sister band of such women is formed perhaps, and a world of good they may do. Trained nurses in hospitals are quite as efficient in the work that is theirs to do, as the well-read physician or the skilful surgeon. As matrons in charge of certain benevolent institutions, the admirable homes provided for the poor and the helpless, the destitute orphan, and the decrepit in advanced years, woman's tact and woman's influence is widely felt—her humble, heavenly faith and tender charity permeating the whole system like leaven hid in meal, and binding all together with the golden link of .Christian love.

As years roll over us, and new avenues of usefulness open, we may see the necessity for many institutions to fit such Christian women as desire to devote themselves to the service of the church, for teachers, and nurses in hospitals, sanatories, and private houses; or to exercise the function of superintendents in female prisons, asylums, homes of refuge, and other charitable establishments where their services may be required.

The most interesting feature perhaps of the labor of the deaconess is the recently developed one of parochial activity. It is the reproduction of the laborers of the early Christian church, of whom Phœbe is the apostolical type. The duty of the parish deaconess is to visit the poor and the sick; to procure for them as far as possible work and clothing; to instruct poor children in sewing and knitting, either singly or in classes, giving a regular account of her labors to the pastor. No doubt this is an admirable plan, as it is one that has already been undertaken by some of our churches to a limited degree. But a few days since I listened to a letter from one of these churches in reference to this work, carried on among them, hitherto by one or two voluntary laborers, but now considered worthy to be organized and supported by the church.

It is not our purpose to enlarge upon this system, neither to decide upon its compatibility with our forms and customs; but rather to speak of woman's work in a social form, as connected with the churches. While it is not given to woman to "usurp authority," it is given her to be the centre of social and domestic life. The family is the nursery of the church, and the Sabbath-school is the intermediate link. The horticulturist gives us to understand that the nursery requires his chief care. In order to have straight trees and a harmonious growth, constant care has to be taken; when they have attained a good degree of strength not so much attention is required; and by-and-by a general oversight is all that is necessary.

The family is the nursery of the church. The church is made up of families, the heads of families the mature members of the church, the children brought into it as soon as they are able to understand what love to Jesus implies, and what trust and confidence in him signify. The great truths of religion are nearer children's hearts than we are usually aware. Simply to love Jesus and to obey him is more readily understood by them, and far easier to be done, than by the man of mature intellect, and inclinations strongly set in the ways of sin. It is a mistake to which the church is just awaking, that children must be shut out; at least, that they must wait a prescribed number of years before they can savingly believe that Jesus Christ, the Son of God, came down to earth, and suffered and died, to redeem them from sin. What is required? Is it anything more than love to Jesus? First love, and then obedience. It is not given woman in general to dazzle by her genius, neither to enlighten through philosophy; but it is given her to do what genius and philosophy fail to accomplish, namely, to win hearts.

Love is the basis of family relations; love is the basis of church union; love is the element of woman's life; love is the atmosphere in which children live. A mother's love, a mother's influence is woven into our very natures. This sentiment is not peculiar to Christian mothers and Christian families. Alexander's mother was a proud, ambitious woman, not inclined simply to live in state when it was known that she was the mother of Alexander; and in her efforts to usurp authority, she was always plunging him into trouble. On one occasion, one of his chief officers and most intimate associates took occasion to speak of this, and to advise him so to limit her power that she could not longer annoy him. The great general replied that, sorely as his mother troubled him, one tear from her overcame it all. This man, that had little mercy for individuals, and none for nations, loved his mother.

Love begets influence. It is through this channel that woman wins; and when her heart is warm with love to Jesus, is there anything to forbid the use of all her faculties of mind, her sweet persuasiveness, to win hearts for her Saviour? Must she tone down her beaming countenance to an unnatural gravity, lessen her charms by using a quaint, unbecoming style of dress and appearance, lay aside that sweet urbanity of manner, the charming fascination of look, word, and deed, because she loves Jesus? Love to Christ is the crowning grace of woman; it is the perfection of womanly beauty. In the room of rendering her less fascinating, it makes her more winning, more worthy of human regard.

It has been said that woman knows not herself until she loves. Doubtless this is true; and it may as truthfully be said that woman is not perfect as a woman, not as noble, not as true, not as lovely as it is in her nature to be, until her heart is filled with love to God.

Love in her heart begets a spirit of

activity. There is no sacrifice that she is not willing to make, no hardship that she cannot endure. There is no barrier in her way, no obstacle that she will not surmount. This principle of love to Christ intensifies her very soul. It is the fountain from which she draws continual supplies; her life is permeated by the breath of the Beloved; and thus beautified, woman becomes a powerful agent in the church of Christ, an active, earnest, working member.

How is this done? Through her influence as a woman in her home, in society, in the street, in the cars. Wherever she is, she is the beautiful charming woman, always ready with a smile, a word of encouragement, a pressure of the hand. Winning hearts for Christ: it is her work. Her energies are alive; she keeps it before her; she has a plan. "Go work to-day in my vineyard," is the command urging her forward. This is a working age: the mind of man is constantly projecting some new plan. Every faculty is employed to win success; wealth, fame, the fleeting honors of an hour are pursued with unwearied diligence. Viewing life as the Christian woman views it, shall she be less active? Is it for her to let golden opportunities pass? Go work, for the night cometh, and the account must be given in. Plain, wise, kindly, and practical she must be, building over against wherever she is, searching out the poor and the suffering, bending over the couch of pain, smoothing with her cool fingers the feverish throbbing brow, gathering up the ignorant and neglected, and telling them of Jesus—is not this effective church work? Will not such efforts win as truly as the sermon from the pulpit, or the labors of the church officers? In the names given of those who built the walls of Jerusalem, mention is made of the daughters as actuated by the same noble love, and actually engaged in the glorious work. The church has walls to be built up. It may not be much that woman can do, only a brick here and there; or it may be some beautiful frescoes, on which an artist is not able to advance more than a hand's breadth in a day. Whatever it is, let it be her best, and God will look on her lowly labors with complacency.

Not only this. Woman is a doctrinal teacher. There are spheres where her teaching secures a wide interest and makes a deep impression. It is probably a mistake that, as Christians, we make so little of the humanity of Christ. When men preach of him as an abstract good, a great unseen power, a glorious being whose throne is in the heavens, what idea does the child gain? Awe and terror may oppress him, but his soul does not open to love. God is to him a God of power, more ready to destroy than to bless him. But tell him of Jesus, tell him of the babe cradled in the manger, point him to the star, show him the wise men as they bow before the babe with their offering of gold, frankincense, and myrrh; tell him that Jesus was once a child, that he had to learn to walk and to speak, that he was obedient to his parents; tell him of this, and you awaken his sympathy, his soul is aroused, love is kindled. Show him Jesus at twelve years of age teaching in the temple, describe to him the anxiety of his parents when they had gone a day's journey towards home, and the boy Jesus was not with them; show him that Mary felt as you would feel if you should lose your little son in a crowd, his little active mind begins to stir and question.

Jesus is real. The boy can think of him just as he thinks of his associates and playfellows. Take him to the wedding at Cana; let him look at the water blushing into wine. Child as he is, he begins to comprehend that Jesus had power that an ordinary man has not. Show him the feeding of the multitude with a few small loaves and fishes. Tell him that Jesus loved Mary and Martha and Lazarus, and that at the grave of Lazarus he wept with them. Make it plain to him how the stone was rolled away, and Jesus standing cried with a loud voice, "Lazarus, come forth." He knows that physicians are sent for to heal the sick, and he also knows that when the sick die and are buried, they never come back again except at the bidding of Christ. Let him understand that Jesus came to earth to suffer and to die for him; and he gains a better idea of the power, as well as of the mercy and loving-kindness of God, than he could get from any other source.

Go through with each of the miracles, and you will be surprised at the interest manifested by the youngest child. Then take him to the garden; but remember the child's heart is susceptible. You must not picture *all* that Christ suffered; you can only tell a part. There are tears in his eyes, indignation on his cheeks, his small hands are clinched. "How could they do it!" he cries. And your voice is lost, the tears are rolling over your own cheeks, you who have known the story so long.

We need not fear making too much of the humanity of Christ. Not only children, but older persons fail to have a real and sensible idea of the God-man. They do not think of him as really a man as they are. His suffering does not move them, perhaps because the idea strikes them that, if really possessed of divine power, he did not suffer. To teach this cardinal truth is appropriately woman's work. It is the alphabet of what is taught in the pulpit, and is not unfrequently overlooked, for the simple reason that it is believed to be sufficiently understood. A talented clergyman, when asked why he did not preach it more fully from the pulpit, replied that he could teach it more effectually in the parlor.

There is still another doctrinal point that comes within woman's domain—a plain practical teaching in reference to the work of the Holy Spirit. A great many professing Christians, it is to be feared, know little of this. They understand something of Christ and the atonement made for sin; but about the inward work of the Spirit they seem profoundly ignorant. Not unfrequently the work of the Spirit is confounded with the action of conscience. The work of the Spirit in the heart leads to repentance and faith in the Lord Jesus Christ. Satan is always ready to assail the truth. Right views on this subject can be disseminated in the parlor as well as in the pulpit. The Spirit is with us as Christ's representative "until he come." The dwelling-place of the Spirit is in our hearts. We are renewed and sanctified, led and taught by the Spirit. Prayer, importunate and ceaseless, is needful for the outpouring of the Spirit. John taught that there is such a thing as the baptism of the Holy Ghost. He taught that it was the especial office of our Lord to give this baptism to men. Forgiveness of sin is not the only thing necessary to salvation. There must be the work of Christ for us, and there must be the work of the Holy Spirit in us. Christ ransomed us by his blood; but the renewing of the soul, growth in grace, and preparation for heaven are wrought in us by the Spirit.

There are distinctive characteristics by which we can know if the Spirit of God dwells in our hearts as a quickening power. By nature we are inactive, torpid, dead; we have not faith, nor hope, nor fear, nor love; we are alive to the world and its pleasures, but dead toward God. The Spirit awakens, renovates, and makes us new creatures in Christ Jesus.

It is the Spirit that enables us to take of the things of Christ and show them unto others. Do we love to do this? Do we find it easy to talk of Jesus in the parlor and by the way? Do we love to commune with him as with a loved and cherished friend? Do we trust with a sweet restful feeling, knowing that a

Father's care is round about us—that we have a precious Elder Brother upon whose arm we can lean? Is it our meat and our drink to work for him?

There are still other points where a woman's tact and ability can mould and fashion others. Order and system belong especially to woman. Let her put every duty in its place, and thus time will be saved and work accomplished. Zealous for Christ's cause, it is hers to uphold the church, and to speak of its ordinances and its ministry with honor. It has been the fashion of some who profess godliness to underrate and attempt to make ridiculous people whose Christian convictions lead them to adopt certain ideas not altogether harmonizing with the etiquette of the times, but in no wise to be held up before the world in such a way as to render the native grace and ability of the careless and indifferent only more attractive, by juxtaposition with the alleged defects of professors of religion. In this way reproach is brought upon religion, and the cause of our Lord is wounded in the house of his friends.

Besides false representations of Christianity, the ministry is held in so little esteem that even mothers scout the idea of their sons entering the service of the church. A few evenings since a mother said, in speaking of her son, and what she would like to have him become, should he grow to manhood, "anything but a minister." "Why so? I would rather see my son a good, faithful minister of the Lord Jesus, than to see him the crowned head of the earth without the qualities necessary for that position," was the reply. There was a puzzled expression on the lovely face of the former, but she said nothing.

To help rectify public opinion, and turn it into better channels, is essentially woman's work. Let the young and beautiful girl give her Christian friend of the other sex to understand that she esteems and reveres those who are willing to make sacrifices for Christ. Her opinion will have its influence.

Not many years since, the writer knew of such an instance. A young man with more than ordinary endowments, and with piety that strongly inclined him to preach Christ and him crucified, had a female friend whom he regarded beyond all others. Before he could decide, he must confer with her. The lady was a member of the same church; but wealth, political fame, and literary eminence were to her far more attractive than the work of the Christian ministry. She could not make up her mind to become a pastor's wife. Alas for the young man called upon to decide between the creature and the Creator. His choice must be made. It was made; and to-day he is a third-rate lawyer, a broken-hearted, spiritless man. His idol was mortal; his house is desolate.

The field is large. Every grade of mental endowment can be brought into use; the tract distributor, the trained teacher, the skilful nurse, and the home-loving girl, according as God has given them, each in her own place building up her part of the wall. God is the disposer of our circumstances as well as of nations; not a sparrow falls to the ground without his notice. The place we each fill is the place that he would have us fill. The question is not how great will be the results, but what effort we make, the spirit in which we work, the self-denial and the love we manifest.

That which approaches nearest to God is the most natural. To do good, do as Jesus did. There was no undeviating form with him. We are told that he "went about doing good." Neither was there any prescribed form in coming to him. Some came of their own accord; some were brought in the arms of their friends; some were let down through the roof. To reach him was the main thing, to behold him the chief desire—to hear him speak, to feel the healing influence running through all their members. Those that loved him followed him, talked of him, were instructed by him, labored for him and with him. Is there any better rule for us?

Again, a Christian woman is in every sense a missionary. True, she may not be called to leave her family and go to the ends of the earth to teach Christ. But if not called to the foreign field, she is to act as a home missionary, "beginning at Jerusalem" at her own home, and working outward as her means, her circumstances, her ability will permit. The sweet graces of her character shine the brightest when seen in the humblest paths. The truths of religion strike the deepest when exemplified by the young and the lovely, at home, in the Sabbath-school, in the street seeking the lost and the miserable. Not with cold formality, but with a sweet feeling of friendliness entering into the details of ordinary life, showing an equality of feeling, of sympathy, of love. The heart that loves Jesus loves those for whom Jesus died. It is a good, true, honest love. Never be afraid to show it. Never be restrained for fear it will not be understood. If Jesus had been afraid of this, he would not have left his Father's throne to come down to us, to show how much he loved us.

Hearts are everywhere the same. Kindness is sure to win.

As an instance, I may be allowed to mention the case of a young disciple, since gone to her gracious reward. Her father was a merchant of great wealth and established integrity of character. His clerks were numerous, young men of fine ability; but not one of them entered his employ with any thought in reference to a future life. This daughter had been carefully educated by a pious mother. She was well read, fascinating in looks and appearance, and as the acknowledged heiress of great wealth, she was a leader in the social circle. Flattered by the crowd, she did not swerve from the sweet faith of her childhood; independent, she did not allow herself to be fettered by the opinions of the weak and the frivolous. She knew enough of the world to know that a young man in the city must be subject to manifold temptations, and she felt that in a certain sense she was responsible for those in her father's employ.

To feel the sweet prompting of duty was to act upon it. Going to her father, she made known to him her plan. At first the merchant was unwilling. Young, beautiful, and rich, he did not care to have his daughter associate with his clerks. But the gentle pleading of his child finally overcame his objections. He had never denied her wishes; he could not now. The result was that the clerks, in the room of being left to spend their leisure time as they best could, were invited to the home of their employer, and by him and by his child were introduced to suitable companions; furnished with books, with a general care and oversight that roused their energies, and led them to cultivate a higher tone of moral character, and to be more faithful to the duties in which they were engaged. Self-respect was deepened. There was a future before them. They were to show themselves men. Thought began to stir and question; and to-day five of those very clerks fill the pulpit, won to preach through the influence of that young Christian girl.

Was not that work quite as effective as any that can be done in the church? Was it less praiseworthy because it was done by one young, beautiful, and rich? Let each labor according as she hath opportunity; and in the harvest time coming from the north and from the south, from the east and from the west, each shall bring her sheaves, and receive the welcome, "Well done, good and faithful servant; .... enter thou in the joy of thy Lord."

www.ingramcontent.com/pod-product-compliance
Lightning Source LLC
LaVergne TN
LVHW010212110826
845151LV00004B/1065

9781425528645